False Feedback in Economics

This book investigates why economics makes less visible progress over time than scientific fields with a strong practical component, where interactions with physical technologies play a key role. The thesis of the book is that the main impediment to progress in economics is "false feedback", which it defines as the false result of an empirical study, such as empirical evidence produced by a statistical model that violates some of its assumptions. In contrast to scientific fields that work with physical technologies, false feedback is hard to recognize in economics. Economists thus have difficulties knowing where they stand in their inquiries, and false feedback will regularly lead them in the wrong directions.

The book searches for the reasons behind the emergence of false feedback. It thereby contributes to a wider discussion in the field of metascience about the practices of researchers when pursuing their daily business. The book thus offers a case study of metascience for the field of empirical economics.

The main strength of the book are the numerous smaller insights it provides throughout. The book delves into deep discussions of various theoretical issues, which it illustrates by many applied examples and a wide array of references, especially to philosophy of science. The book puts flesh on complicated and often abstract subjects, particularly when it comes to controversial topics such as p-hacking.

The reader gains an understanding of the main challenges present in empirical economic research and also the possible solutions. The main audience of the book are all applied researchers working with data and, in particular, those who have found certain aspects of their research practice problematic.

Andrin Spescha is a postdoctoral researcher at ETH Zurich, KOF Swiss Economic Institute, Zurich, Switzerland. He received his PhD from ETH Zurich (Dr. sc. ETH) in 2018. Prior to this, he completed a Bachelor of Arts in Political Sciences and Economics and a Master of Arts in Economics at the University of Zurich, Switzerland.

Routledge Studies in Economic Theory, Method and Philosophy

False Feedback in Economics
The Case for Replication
Andrin Spescha

For more information about this series, please visit: www.routledge.com/ Routledge-Studies-in-Economic-Theory-Method-and-Philosophy/ book-series/RSEMTP

False Feedback in Economics

The Case for Replication

Andrin Spescha

Routledge
Taylor & Francis Group

LONDON AND NEW YORK

First published 2022
by Routledge
2 Park Square, Milton Park, Abingdon, Oxon OX14 4RN

and by Routledge
605 Third Avenue, New York, NY 10158

Routledge is an imprint of the Taylor & Francis Group, an informa business

British Library Cataloguing-in-Publication Data
A catalogue record for this book is available from the British Library

Library of Congress Cataloging-in-Publication Data
Names: Spescha, Andrin, author.
Title: False feedback in economics: the case for replication / Andrin Spescha.
Description: 1 Edition. | New York: Routledge, 2021. |
Series: Routledge studies in economic theory, method and philosophy |
Includes bibliographical references and index.
Identifiers: LCCN 2021005622 (print) | LCCN 2021005623 (ebook)
Subjects: LCSH: Economics–Methodology. | Economics–Research. |
Feedback (Psychology) | Reinforcement (Psychology)
Classification: LCC HB131.S65 2021 (print) |
LCC HB131 (ebook) | DDC 330.01/595–dc23
LC record available at https://lccn.loc.gov/2021005622
LC ebook record available at https://lccn.loc.gov/2021005623

ISBN: 978-1-032-03371-6 (hbk)
ISBN: 978-1-032-03372-3 (pbk)
ISBN: 978-1-003-18699-1 (ebk)

Typeset in Sabon
by Newgen Publishing UK

To all PhD students out there

Contents

Introduction

This book provides a comprehensive account of the challenges empirical economics faces. It explains approaches used implicitly by most researchers and shows where they are adequate and where they break down. The aim of the book is to provide applied researchers with an understanding of these challenges and how best to overcome them. Only an in-depth understanding of the specific challenges will allow taking the right measures to solve them, as the understanding itself paves the way toward the right solutions. After reading the book, applied researchers of every standing should be aware of the causes of and of the ways to address the challenges present in today's empirical economics.

The book illustrates the problems of empirical research in economics in their manifold appearances. The style of the book is to delve deeply into theoretical concepts and mechanisms, to bring them to light by thinking them through from different angles. This puts flesh on multifaceted issues like p-hacking and brings often abstract concepts to life. The contribution of the book is a framework that connects together these different problems in their various forms. It does so in a practice-oriented way and illustrates its main ideas with references to philosophy and metascience as well as with actual examples taken from daily research activity.

The audience of the book is in principle everyone working in empirical research in the fields of economics, business, finance, etc. This includes everyone working in the private sector. Key is only that the reader has worked with data, will work with data, or is interested in working with data. An undergraduate degree in any of those fields is sufficient to understand the book. Younger researchers can probably profit most from the outlined contents, as they can still adapt their research practices accordingly, or are at least aware of potential shortfalls right from the outset of their careers.

More specifically, the book is targeted at all those applied empirical researchers, who, like me, have sensed issues in their own research, but could never fully grasp, let alone adequately express them. I hope this book will help them in organizing their thoughts about the sometimes confusing world of empirical research and provide them with support to uncover potential problems. In my own research I fell myself prey to many of the problematic practices I will outline in this book, mostly because I did not know any better. I began to grasp their critical nature only with time and in the course of writing this book. Ex-post, my own research was more like a school where I learned after every project what not to do, but of course always only after I had run upfront into every thinkable error.

Sometime during my PhD, I perceived the state of economics as so problematic that it led me straight into Pyrrhonian skepticism. Because I was not able to know, I tried to suspend all judgment and to focus on more applied things. The skeptics argue that the value you get in exchange for suspending judgment is quietude. The less you know about a subject, the less you have to worry about it, which results in peace of mind. For some months, I was so knee-deep in skepticism about economics that I considered going back to university and studying a subject with a more applied focus, a practical profession like engineering, medicine, or even law. I guess skepticism is the frustrated outburst of all disoriented truth-seekers like me, so they can opt for at least one, eternal certainty, namely, that "we do not know", and then hold on to this one certainty very tightly. Ironically, a true Pyrrhonian skeptic would not even grant this certainty, as he or she would say that we do not know whether we do not know. To state that I know that I do not know is dogmatic again. This latter argument was in the end also what brought me back on track. Instead of giving up on economics, I wanted to find a way out and started to think about the possible reasons why I perceived economics as being in such a problematic state. This effort, which stretched over a period of more than four years, led me to write this book.

The book serves as a complement for the more traditional textbooks in econometrics. Research methods beyond the standard econometrics toolkit are typically taught in an informal fashion during the supervision of research papers. Unfortunately, this informal teaching is part of the problem, too, as many questionable research practices are thought from advisers to students, where sometimes neither of them realizes that they are in fact questionable. Many researchers are not yet aware of the extent to which they are engaging in problematic practices. We need more formal engagement with controversial topics such as p-hacking and their possible solutions. Active discussions about them should be part of every graduate research curriculum. The book thus opens up a debate in empirical economics that is long overdue given much of the daily practice of most applied researchers.

A close companion of the book is Christensen et al. (2019) (see also Miguel al. [2014] and Christensen and Miguel [2018]), who provide an overview of potential solutions to address many of the issues raised in this book. This book will take up potential solutions in the last five chapters. In contrast to Christensen et al. (2019), the book will put the main emphasis on portraying the problems present in empirical economics. To be able to implement the right measures, we need to fully grasp the underlying problems first. Moreover, without understanding the problems, only few economists will be willing to act and implement solutions accordingly. Economics first needs forceful wakeup calls.

The book cites various contributions from the field of metascience, especially when they help to better flesh out and describe the respective issues in economics. However, the intention of the book is not to provide a summary of all potentially relevant studies present in the field of metascience. Hardwicke et al. (2019), for instance, give such an overview; they describe the developments in metascience by categorizing the contributions of the growing literature. This book, in contrast, tries to distill the core theoretical contents relevant for economics that this by now large literature provides.

The book is structured into four separate parts. The first three chapters set the stage for the entire book. They lay out the overarching theme that connects everything together. The key question of Chapter 1 is why progress is so uneven between different scientific fields. It argues that false feedback, which it defines as a false empirical answer, is the key to understand this puzzle. Chapter 2 lays out how false feedback relates to trial and error, the engine behind much of the progress we observe not only in science but also in practical tasks like programing. Chapter 3 discusses how researchers obtain their trials and how, from the viewpoint of philosophy of science, they can learn from the obtained errors. It concludes that before we can pursue any inference, we need reliable testing.

Chapters 4–7 constitute the core of the book. They explain how false feedback emerges in empirical research. Chapter 4 argues that the large discretionary room researchers have in specifying their empirical strategy, the so-called researcher degrees of freedom, are the main culprit behind false feedback. They allow researchers too many arbitrary methodological choices, which together result in large variation in the obtained feedback. Chapter 5 relates the numerous alternative choices researchers have to the Duhem–Quine thesis from philosophy of science. Seen in this light, false feedback is the result of a reliance on false auxiliary hypotheses. Chapter 6 discusses how practices like p-hacking, which exploits researcher degrees of freedom to achieve statistical significance, make the problem of false feedback worse. In fact, much of the false feedback in economics is a direct result of these practices. Chapter 7 explains the process of how we mistakenly perceive false feedback as true feedback. This "illusion of true feedback" makes it difficult for researchers to identify true empirical findings.

Chapters 8–10 lay out the consequences of false feedback for the scientific literature. Chapter 8 describes how researchers relying on false empirical results can drift into a "false feedback bubble", which means that the direction of research deviates from empirical reality in unpredictable ways. Chapter 9 portrays the difficulties researchers have in coherently organizing studies corresponding to false feedback. Chapter 10 argues that before we can tackle further issues such as external validity, we need more reliably true feedback, which, in addition, might prove favorable for public policy.

The last four chapters provide possible solutions for the issue of false feedback. Chapter 11 contrasts empirical research with machine learning applied to practical tasks. It points out that economics could profit from the sample split approaches common in machine learning. Chapter 12 raises the possibility of a stronger connection of research to daily economic life. This could provide not just new theoretical insights but would help in sorting out unrealistic theories. Chapter 13 discusses robustness checks, a practice already common in empirical economics. It argues that they are not sufficient to tackle the problem of false feedback. Finally, Chapter 14 proposes potential solutions to combat false feedback in economics. The effectiveness of each solution thereby emerges naturally from the previous content of the book. The chapter argues for replication as the most promising solution.

1   Scientific progress

The central question of this book is why economics makes less visible progress over time than scientific fields with a strong practical component, where interactions with physical technologies play a key role. Every attentive student of economics will eventually wonder why we observe progress in the form of highly advanced technologies everywhere, whereas the science of economics, where analysis of the use of these technologies plays such a central role, shows in comparison much fewer visible progress. Applied scientists develop more skillful robots, more sophisticated software, and more powerful computers, which together make up the technological innovations that are an essential ingredient to the growth of our economies. Economists, on the other hand, are mainly concerned with contributing always new studies to a disordered literature of existing studies, making it difficult to evaluate whether there is progress or not. As an economist, it seems thus natural to ask: why do *economies* advance so rapidly but *economics* does much less so? Why does the knowledge embodied in applied technologies grow so fast, while knowledge of the field of economics grows much slower in comparison? This question is extremely relevant, because many young and able economists leave the field precisely due to this discrepancy. They desert to fields such as the computer sciences, which has a strong practical component, building on applied technologies, and has thus experienced immense progress over the last decades.

To observe the disorder present in the economic literature, one merely needs to read a large number of published articles on any important economic question. The findings of these articles will be hard to reconcile and too often seem outright contradictory. Every researcher who wrote an honest literature review on any relevant economic topic will agree that most published articles are not compatible with each other. They form complicated overlappings that are hard to fit into a sensibly organized whole. Together, the articles should form a large and well-arranged puzzle; instead, they rather constitute a large pile of lost pieces. Of course, economists do not always talk past each other. They agree on certain fundamental principles, such as the enormous power inherent to the market system, the equilibrating forces of supply and demand. However, these principles are so self-evident to most economists that there exists only few research on them; they rather play the role of core assumptions upon which the entire economic discipline builds on. In contrast, if we go beyond these most fundamental principles, we observe almost no unambiguous answers in the literature on any important question. For example, we have way too many equally reasonable explanations for key economic phenomena such as the business cycle, economic growth, or income inequality; every economist will name a different set of explanations as the most important ones in understanding their emergence.

This book argues that the main reason behind the more limited progress in economics is "false feedback". False feedback is a false answer that appears to be true. For instance, when researchers obtain an empirical result to answer a certain question that appears true to other researchers, and too often even to themselves, even though it is actually false. Unfortunately, economics is abound with studies that correspond to such false feedback. The presence of false feedback makes it difficult to achieve progress in any scientific field. Knowledge can only grow when researchers are able to rely on true feedback; they need true answers about how their proposed hypotheses compare against empirical reality. If researchers obtain false answers to their questions, and are not able to also recognize them as such, they will have a wrong understanding of where exactly they are standing in their inquiries. False feedback will regularly mislead them to move into the wrong directions.

People pursuing practical tasks can generally profit from repeated true feedback. They receive true answers to the "questions" they pose to nature. For instance, if a programmer feeds his computer with a code line, it either runs through or results in error. The computer produces a true answer whether the respective code has worked out or not. The programmer faces no ambiguity about the success or failure of his coding trials; he always knows exactly where he is at. If the code results in error, the programmer has to rewrite it and submit a new trial. The constant error messages are the element enabling him to achieve progress, step-by-step. They guide the programmer toward a solution that will work out. And the more trials he has pursued in his career, the better he will be able to achieve his desired targets. Every technology, where working on it corresponds to such a practical task producing true feedback, makes fast progress possible. Whenever practitioners receive true answers whether the steps they took in creating their objects work out or not, they can readily achieve progress.

To be able to investigate the idea of false feedback more closely, however, we need a more rigorous definition. I define feedback in economics as the result one gets back from the empirical test of a hypothesis. To define both true and false feedback, I rely on a correspondence theory of truth (David 2016). Feedback is true if and only if it corresponds to the facts, meaning that the empirical test produces results equal to the way how things really are. Feedback is false if it does not correspond to the facts; the empirical results deviate from the way how things really are. More specifically, I define true feedback as empirical evidence produced by a statistical model that satisfies all of its assumptions. I define false feedback as empirical evidence produced by a statistical model that violates some of its assumptions. False feedback is thus a deviation of the applied statistical model from the true state of things; it does not adequately represent economic reality, too often without explicitly showing it.

Research essentially follows a structure of trial and error (Popper 1963). The development of a new hypothesis corresponds to a trial, whereas the feedback produced by an empirical test corresponds to the response that decides whether the trial is in error or not. Similarly, I define feedback in practical tasks as the response one receives during a process of trial and error. Whether feedback can be designated as true or false, however, depends on the knowledge one has about the state of things before the trial. For instance, an applied scientist working on a technology needs to know the setup that led up to the trial very well, otherwise she will not be able to distill true feedback. In many practical tasks, true feedback is the rule and false feedback is the exception. If an applied scientist works on a technology, the properties of the technology show themselves openly to her. The real world presents itself directly to the applied scientist; she does not have to rely on (hidden) assumptions about the technology. In the words of Popper (1976), the applied scientist is aware of all the relevant background knowledge. Because she knows the setup of the technology right before the trial, if the trial fails, she knows why the trial has failed. Conversely, if the trial is successful, she knows that her setup was correct. As long as the applied scientist knows everything of relevance that went into the trial, she will be able to extract true feedback. The knowledge of the state of things before the trial allows constructing a correct account of how the trial relates to the outcome. Importantly, unlike in economics, the applied scientist cannot misrepresent how the world really is; the physical proper-ties of the technology are what they are and she cannot violate them in the same way as the economist can violate crucial assumptions. I thus define true feedback in practical tasks as a true account of why a trial has worked out or not. In contrast, false feedback in practical tasks emerges only if the applied scientist is not well informed about the current state of the tech-nology, due to, for instance, a misunderstanding or too high complexity. If she does not know how exactly the technology works, she will attribute a failure or success to the wrong properties of the technology. I thus define false feedback in practical tasks as a false account of why a trial has worked out or not.

In practical tasks, the resistance of the physical technology itself allows for the true feedback. Whereas the individual components of the tech-nology can be freely dissected and recombined, the nature of the indi-vidual components cannot be altered; they remain what they are, and physical laws set the boundaries here. Unlike assumptions in empirical work in economics, their particular properties cannot be violated. All that is necessary to receive true feedback in practical tasks is knowledge of how the individual components relate to each other. The deeper this knowledge, the more precise the true feedback will be. In applied economics, in contrast, researchers face no resistance from the data when violating assumptions of the statistical model. Many important details of the real-world context within which the respective assumptions are integrated remain hidden, such that researchers often do not even recognize when they have violated some of the assumptions of their statistical models. Consequently, very often researchers are not aware that they have just produced false feedback.

Sciences where practical work with physical technologies constitutes an essential element thus achieve much faster progress than sciences where such a close link to physical reality is missing. This concerns not only economics, but also, for instance, sociology, political sciences, or psychology. All of these sciences cannot profit from the true feedback that physical technologies allow for and have to rely on empirical modeling using data, which lacks such an immediate connection to physical reality.

Nelson (2003) similarly argues that practical know-how and scientific understanding are most advanced in fields where there is a focus on technologies that allow for experimentation relevant to both of these domains. Working on the technology must produce results applicable to what is pursued in practice and what is investigated in science. If the technology allows for a trial and error process that generates true feedback, advances in both practical know-how and scientific understanding are feasible. In such a case, technology and scientific understanding evolve together. The development of a new technology enables new scientific understanding that goes beyond the new technology, while this new understanding in turn provides inputs for the further development of again new technologies. Progress happens through an iterative search process moving back and forth between on-line (practice) and off-line (scientific work) (Nelson 2003). It is the nature of the technology itself that determines to what degree we can achieve advances in practical know-how and scientific understanding. If, when worked on, the technology produces true feedback allowing for joint application in both daily practice and scientific work, the two mutually reinforce each other, with fast progress as the result for both.

Take, for instance, the computer sciences, where doing and thinking are strongly interwoven. The theoretical study of algorithms, computation, and information moves hand in hand with new applications in hardware and software, which are practical tasks that rely heavily on the process of trial-and-error. Newly developed methods are tested out in practice, and those fields where practical application proves most successful are also those fields that progress fastest. For instance, the field of machine learning has also developed so fast because it offers many very useful practical applications (see also, e.g., Gelman and Vehtari (2020), who argue that in statistics in general theory motivates application and vice versa; if removed from its source of nourishment, theory dries up like a plucked apple).

Progress in applied sciences that rely on practical tasks is usually directly visible, for instance in the construction of a new prototype that outperforms all previous prototypes. Progress in economics is much harder to pin down. I define it as an improvement in the match between theory and reality. This definition assumes scientific realism; there exists an independent reality out there we can learn about (Chakravartty 2017). More specifically, it again assumes a correspondence theory of truth, meaning that a theory is true if and only if it corresponds to the facts. Given scientific realism, correct scientific methods, that is, those methods yielding true feedback, would eventually lead to an uncovering of (at least approximately) true theories. In terms of logic, this definition of progress in economics corresponds to an increase in verisimilitude, which means an increase in the truth content of a theory (Popper 1972). The challenge to this definition is of course the measurement whether the match between theory and reality has improved or not. However, while the agreement between different empirical results does not necessarily imply correspondence to truth, widespread disagreement between results impedes an increase in truth content; if we have a myriad of largely incompatible "facts", we have no way of knowing whether our theories indeed approach truth or not. If we have difficulties in choosing what empirical results to rely on, what agrees and what contrasts with our theories, we cannot reliably diagnose errors, and there are consequently few hopes for progress. In the presence of false feedback, contributing to the literature becomes difficult or even impossible. Did we merely face false feedback? Which of the existing studies are true and which are false? And can we be sure about this?

The core problem is that the vast majority of studies in economics are incomparable, which creates difficulties in evaluating their conclusions against each other, and one does not know whether they agree or contradict each other. Most studies are incomparable because, even if they test the very same theory, they are based on different hypotheses, empirical strategies, and environments, with the consequence that findings fall all over the place. These discrepancies in the setup of studies create intricate interplays leading to large variation in the obtained feedback. If studies are incomparable, we do not even know whether their findings are in fact disputed or not. Even if studies agree, we do not know why they agree. Although a great many studies approach true feedback quite well, the difficulty is to recognize them as such among the midst of all studies constituting false feedback. False feedback lets us believe that effects are present when they are not and vice versa, and that effects are smaller or larger than they in fact are. The implication is a huge literature without much sensible connections, which can only be organized by selective, and often subjective, choices.

The term feedback is in economic research usually reserved for inputs from colleagues, other researchers, or journal reviewers. This type of feedback will play a lesser role in the book. The knowledge base in economics certainly also depends to a large extent on critical exchange at conferences, the review process, and the scrutiny of the follow-up literature. This intellectual competition leads to important checks and balances helping economics to keep track. However, these aspects are so important in economics because our studies produce too much false feedback. An unambiguous empirical result, like the discovery of the Higgs boson in physics, does not require further discussions among researchers. The issue is settled by a single (albeit huge) project. Inputs from other researchers help us in not losing our focus, but they cannot substitute for rigorous empirical testing. The focus of the book therefore lies on the type of feedback that provides the most important basis for criticism in economics: the empirical results researchers obtain through the use of statistical tests. The results of our empirical tests correspond to the feedback that would in principle allow us settling open questions about our economic hypotheses. To settle questions, we need facts, and only empirical results can provide us with them. Inputs from other researchers can certainly correct the false feedback we receive from empirical studies to some degree, but they cannot guarantee that feedback indeed better approaches truth. Only a fundamental change in the way we generate our empirical results can do so. A discussion of the mechanisms allowing for check and balances in economics would also dive heavily into the sociology of scientific knowledge. This book, in contrast, is about the particular problem of false feedback and how it hinders progress in economics. It is certainly not the only factor inhibiting progress, but the most fundamental one. Unambiguous true feedback in economics would make most critical discussions superfluous, as we would have clear empirical answers to our open questions.

In his seminal book "The structure of scientific revolution", Kuhn (1962) gives an account of scientific progress quite different from that of Karl Popper. For Kuhn the essential element of every science is the process of normal science. Kuhn (1962) describes normal science as a collective "puzzle-solving". Normal science is an "attempt to force nature into the preformed and relatively inflexible boxes that the paradigm supplies" (Kuhn 1962). The paradigm provides both the puzzles and the corresponding rules on how to solve them. The rules are thereby often tacit, acquired through scientific practice. Over time, the advance of normal science, achieved through the collective efforts of scientists, opens up anomalies in the paradigm, that is, puzzles scientists are unable to solve. It is the efficient process of normal science itself that unearths problems with the paradigm. When the anomalies become unbearable, science enters into a crisis and alternative paradigms start to appear. Eventually, a scientific revolution starts, and the scientific community transitions to a new paradigm (Kuhn 1962).

Mayo (1996a) recasts this standard Kuhnian picture of science and portrays it as a collective trial and error process, closer in spirit again to Karl Popper. Normal science delivers the means necessary for severe testing. The more stringent the testing is during normal science, the more reliably it can detect anomalies that show where the paradigm breaks down. Hence, the collective efforts of scientists during normal science produce rigorous trials, which, if they repeatedly result in error, provide the basis for the transition to a new paradigm. In contrast to Kuhn (1962), who describes the transition to a new paradigm as a "conversion", Mayo (1996a) argues that experimental testing provides the crucial link between the detection of anomalies and the shift to a new paradigm. It presents the means for the collective trial and error processes to learn and is thus the driver behind scientific progress.

Seen in this light, if we observed only true feedback, a clearly defined set of anomalies would arise in empirical economics, which could show where our theories break down. Economists could then target these anomalies and try to find new theories to resolve them. They would eventually overcome the crisis caused by the anomalies and move economics toward a new paradigm. In contrast, if we observe primarily false feedback, with much of it masking as contradictory empirical evidence, we do not even know whether we face clear anomalies and can thus also not improve our theories.

Several empirical studies have tried to quantify the extent of false feedback in economics. Of course, these empirical meta-studies may suffer from the very same problems as the empirical studies they in turn investigate. Nonetheless, these studies can at least provide some indications that false feedback indeed exists in economics, even though we may not be certain about its exact extent.

Ioannidis et al. (2017) investigate the test statistics from more than 6700 empirical studies published in 159 economic literatures. Using over 64,000 estimates of economic parameters, they conclude that most empirical economic research is severely underpowered. If a study is underpowered and nonetheless shows statistically significant estimates, these will generally be too large. Indeed, Ioannidis et al. (2017) find evidence of strongly inflated effect sizes; nearly 80% of the reported effects are exaggerated, typically by a factor of two, with one-third by a factor of four or more. The study of Ioannidis et al. (2017) would therefore indicate that false feedback is ubiquitous in economics.

Publications in top journals in economics are not exempt from false feedback either. Brodeur et al. (2016) investigate 50,000 tests from articles published in the American Economic Review (AER), the Journal of Political Economy (JPE), and the Quarterly Journal of Economics (QJE) over the period 2005–2011. They find that 10–20 percent of tests below the p-value threshold of 0.05 are misallocated; they would actually belong somewhere in the range of p-values between 0.10 and 0.25. Brodeur et al. (2016) attribute this pattern to the behavior of researchers, who explicitly choose statistically significant specifications and discard insignificant ones. Forcing empirical estimates to achieve statistical significance constitutes a severe form of false feedback we will discuss in Chapter 6.

Some areas of economics seem to be hit particularly hard by false feedback. Harvey et al. (2016) investigate 313 studies published in top journals in finance, economics, and accounting that introduce new factors to explain the cross-section of expected returns in financial markets. They apply a multiple testing framework correcting for the fact that these numerous studies together constitute a large-scale, collective pursuit of data mining. About half of all factors discovered in the 313 studies do not pass the more stringent t-statistic thresholds derived by Harvey et al. (2016), who subsequently conclude that "most claimed research findings in financial economics are likely false".

Even the results of studies relying on laboratory experiments, the gold standard of clean identification, can correspond to false feedback. Camerer et al. (2016) replicate all 18 experimental studies published in the AER and QJE between 2011 and 2014. They find significant effects in the same direction as the original studies in 11 of the 18 cases (61.1%), while on average the replicated effects were only 65.9% of the original sizes. Similarly, Camerer et al. (2018) replicate 21 social science laboratory experiments published in Nature and Science between 2010 and 2015. They find a significant effect in the same direction as the original studies for 13 replications (61.9%), while on average the replicated effects were only 46.2% of the original sizes. Of course, the replication attempts of Camerer et al. (2016, 2018) rely themselves on very small sample sizes. The actual replication rate of economic studies could thus be both much higher or much lower. Nonetheless, they indicate that even the seemingly most rigorous laboratory experiments published in top journals can correspond to false feedback.

Finally, Black et al. (2020) replicate four studies published in top journals in finance and economics investigating a large-scale randomized experiment (Regulation SHO). These four studies are part of a larger literature that finds positive effects of this experiment on various outcomes, even though the underlying theoretical channels are often weak. Black et al. (2020) use a pre-specified sample and research design to constrain them from searching for outcomes. They find no support for the hypotheses proposed in the four studies. When they try to match the samples and specifications of the four studies as close as possible, Black et al. (2020) find that the obtained results are highly sensitive to specification choices and none of them are robust to even minor changes. They thus argue that the four studies most likely represent false discoveries. Black et al. (2020) conclude that the results of the larger literature exploiting this large-scale randomized experiment are likely to fare no better. Hence, there may even be entire literatures whose collective answers correspond to false feedback.

The focus on better research designs in the wake of the "credibility revolution" (Angrist and Pischke 2010) has certainly improved the quality of empirical economics. It moved empirical economics much closer to the scientific ideal of the controlled experiment. Researchers now investigate all sorts of natural experiments, quasi-experiments, and actual experiments like randomized controlled trials (RCTs). However, the pursuit of experiments alone cannot eliminate false feedback. In fact, the discussion whether most research findings are false has started out in fields like medicine (Ioannidis 2005) and psychology (Simmons et al. 2011), where experiments have always been common. Even if the identification strategy of a study is perfect, numerous other aspects can still invalidate it, namely all the wrong choices in the dense jungle of data collection, cleaning, processing, and analysis. The discussion of these so-called researcher degrees of freedom will make up the core content of the book in Chapters 5–7. The book is thus in the spirit of Leamer (1978, 1983, 1985), whose concerns about the arbitrariness inherent to the setup of empirical studies in economics have not been fully addressed even after forty years. Or as Leamer (1983) puts it: "The fundamental problem facing econometrics is how adequately to control the whimsical character of inference, how sensibly to base inferences on opinions when facts are unavailable". Researchers still retain too much, or even more, leeway in their empirical analyses, allowing them countless arbitrary decisions responsible for most of the false feedback.

However, before we can tackle the main reasons behind the emergence of false feedback in empirical economics, we will first explore in more detail why practical tasks and thus also sciences that incorporate them are so successful, as this helps to flesh out why true feedback is so important.

2   Trial and error

To understand why practical tasks are so successful is important for understanding progress everywhere. They are a model comparison group where trial and error proves very effective. The idea that all progress develops through a process of repeated trial and error has been put forward most prominently by Sir Karl Raimund Popper (1945, 1957, 1959, 1963, 1972, 1985, 1994). Hence, when we understand why trial and error works well in practical tasks, we can hope to draw lessons as to why in other areas, especially in sciences that lack a direct connection to the physical world, progress is much more limited. One could also compare progress in economics to progress in related fields like sociology, political sciences, or psychology. However, they are less instructive as a comparison group because they suffer from very similar problems as economics. In order to understand how to achieve fast progress, we must look at fields that exhibit strengths which the social sciences are lacking. Practical tasks are instructive here since they are able to reap the full potential of trial and error. The particular processes through which they unfold can further contribute to our understanding why physical technologies and, as a consequence, also sciences that incorporate such technologies can progress this fast.

The most important ingredient for success in every trial and error approach is that it generates true feedback in every step. That is, the process gives back correct information about why the trial has failed or succeeded. This true feedback makes it possible to correct errors and thus to improve constantly. Even experienced practitioners could not progress without always trying out their proposed solutions. Otherwise, the process will result in errors that can be very difficult to correct later on. We need to be able to rely with high confidence on why trials have resulted in errors. To be effective, trial and error requires true feedback; you need to know where exactly you are standing, all the time.

In practical tasks, trial and error delivers true feedback because the person performing it understands the context of the situation he is in. Given his objective, he simply knows whether a trial has worked out or not, and, importantly, because of his grasp of the relevant circumstances, he is able to filter out the reasons why the trial has succeeded or failed. The better he knows the circumstances, the better he will be able to extract true feedback. The knowledge about the context of the exact situation allows him to make this judgment, to isolate the cause responsible for the failure or success of the trial.

Successful trial and error requires small steps, as learning from large steps is difficult. If in a trial many things change simultaneously, it becomes hard to disentangle which of them were responsible for either the trial's success or failure. In order to learn from feedback, changes in the outcome need to be attributable to particular causes. Ideally, trial and error first takes place only at the local level. If it works out, the developed strategy can be applied to a more global level. Similarly, some trials might be difficult to attribute to particular causes, as other factors may play a role as well. In such cases, repeated feedback can pave the way out, as it allows isolating true answers on average.

After the completion of a project, the practitioner has figured out many small steps that work together very well, making up her expertise. In the next project, she can then rely on this expertise and will find solutions much faster. The accumulation of expertise through participating in a large number of different projects makes it possible that in future projects the trial and error process progresses very fast, since the necessary intuition about which steps to take next has already developed.

One might argue that the planning and successful construction of large-scale projects, like for instance entire factories, falsifies the relevance of the small-scale trial and error approach. Popper (1945) objects to this argument that all of the involved architects, engineers, and builders can only complete such a large-scale project because they can rely on their cumulative experience of all previous smaller trial and error projects they have worked on over their lives. Moreover, they can rely on the cumulative successes their professions have achieved over decades of continuous trial and error searches. Compare, for instance, the earliest versions of automobiles with the automobiles we have today. The latter are the result of numerous little improvements we have made in building automobiles over the past century.

In many cases, the starting point of the whole trial and error process does not matter, as the project can be corrected along the way. However, because of path dependency, starting out with more elaborate guesses is favorable. Otherwise, the project may head into the wrong direction for quite some time. Sometimes small decisions made at the outset of a project can have large long-run consequences that are hard to anticipate, as these small decisions turn out to be crucial only in later stages of the project. Such unfortunate instances can make it necessary to completely reconstruct the entire project to set it on a firm basis again.

Noise is a common element in trial and error; feedback can sometimes be very inexact. In the presence of noise, progress becomes slower. In such a case, the time lag between successive feedbacks is decisive. If the feedback is very fast, the practitioner can simply run many different trials to find out where the error originates from. However, to be successful in the presence of noise, trial and error needs to produce feedback that is true at least in expectation; the noise has to be random. If this is the case, fast feedback allows quickly achieving the appropriate solution even if feedback is noisy. In contrast, if feedback is not true in expectation, that is, feedback is consistently false, then fast feedback actually worsens the situation, as trial and error leads very fast into a completely wrong direction.

To enable progress, feedback needs thus not only to exhibit low uncertainty, it also needs to be fast. A practitioner engaged in explorative trial and error does not need to think too many steps ahead. Impulsive creativity is more important than exact thinking. A high number of different trials will allow him to improve nonetheless, and, step-by-step, to build objects of high complexity. The true feedback provided by the material object guides him through the entire trial and error process. Either the trial works out or it does not, the true feedback comes along for free, the only requirement is repeated effort. In contrast, the conduct of research requires huge efforts in rigorous thinking to recognize ahead all potential errors. Nonetheless, some errors will always slip through. This leads to the consequence that a lesser mind engaging in a trial and error task with fast and certain feedback will be much more successful than a genius engaging in a research task with slow and uncertain feedback.

Because of an absence of repeated true feedback, researchers have to plan ahead and construct mental models. They have to reflect in their minds on all possibilities, from all angles, and can detect errors only by rigorous thinking. To understand the difficulty of creating a scientific theory without access to repeated empirical feedback, think about constructing a large-scale lie. Liars need to think through in advance even the smallest eventualities; otherwise, they will fail sooner or later. Most large-scale liars would agree that even their most elaborate systems have broken down at some point, due to unforeseen situations, which is tantamount to empirical feedback proving them wrong. Even though our target is to map reality and not to construct it, research can at times feel like building such a large-scale lie, because when compared to practical tasks, we receive so few true feedback.

To complete a task through trial and error, an overarching objective is necessary. The Prussian Field Marshal Helmuth von Moltke (1800–1891) stated in a famous passage of his work "Über Strategie" that no operational plan will survive the first major encounter with the enemy. Whereas an able general pursues a general objective, the path he will take to achieve it cannot be specified in advance, because he will have to make important decisions about situations he could not possibly have foreseen. Every military campaign requires a clear objective, while the series of actual decisions the general takes is hardly predictable. Numerous decisions to handle the unforeseen situations will result in smaller failures, which then again necessitate further important decisions and so on. In all of this, the general must never forget his general objective. And, just like in every task, the more true feedback the general will receive during the battle, the better he will be able to approach his objective.

The crucial aspect is smart reaction to upcoming failures. The experienced solider quickly realizes how to correct failures or at least how to dampen their consequences and then to set focus on the target again. The very best soldiers even use failures to their own advantage. They are not necessarily perfect executers of a pre-specified plan, but they are adept improvisers who can react as soon as their plan starts to break down and are nevertheless able to complete the set target.

Not all people are made for aggressive trial and error searches though, even when the corresponding errors are relatively small. Some persons suffer from the errors they have committed for quite some time. They turn them around in their heads again and again, sometimes leading to severe psychological distress. Such individuals need to proceed much more cautiously. Importantly, aggressive trial and error is never a good idea if the potential downside is large (Taleb 2007). If the consequences of a trial are potentially catastrophic, even if the probability is very small, one should take cautious and small steps, or even refrain from any trials at all. Trial and error is appropriate only under situations with a limited downside and very appropriate if the potential upside is large.

The problem of research in economics is that when someone has hit on truth, he or she quite often lacks the means to convince skeptics. An engineer can build a prototype in a very unconventional way, with all other engineers agreeing that it will fail because of a false method. Yet if the prototype works, the engineer was right all along, and all the skeptics were wrong; there is no way for them to still doubt it. In economic research, skeptics can simply continue doubting every possible method.

Nelson (2008) argues that researchers can achieve progress through trial and error only when they are able to distinguish in a fine-grained way what the effects of their trials are; they require feedback that is specific, meaning that it is accurate up to a high level of detail. If the feedback is too general, lacking sufficient details, it will not allow the researchers differentiating to what extent a trial has worked out or not. The ability to see in a fine-grained way is essential for progress through trial and error. Nelson (2008) describes it as a researcher having a superior set of glasses. The higher the resolution of the glasses, the better visible the obtained feedback becomes. Nelson (2008) argues that the ability to see to what extent a trial has worked out or not is something that can be taken for granted. For example, he mentions that microbial theory only took off with the instruments and techniques that enabled to actually see microbes. This theory then set the basis for identifying particular microbes involved in diseases, which in turn enabled an even finer-grained perception. To provide a basis for further investigation on our problems, we need the ability to specify closely the exact ways we have previously taken in our work; researchers need a certain amount of reliable details in order to build successfully on the work of their predecessors.

Finally, feedback can also take on the form of careful observation of the world. In economics, the most widely accepted feedback is the infrequent real-life feedback obtained from large-scale historical situations such as, for instance, the Great Depression, after which new classical economics took a severe blow and Keynesian economics started rising. Much falsification of economic theories thus depends on the time lapse between important real-life feedbacks.

In sum, in both processes, practical tasks and economic research, we obtain repeated feedback. However, whereas in many practical tasks the feedback process is fast and certain, in economic research the feedback process is slow and uncertain. In many practical tasks the feedback thus makes rapid progress possible, whereas the feedback process in economics too often leads us astray.

3 Conjectures and falsification

Popper (1972, 1994) describes the process of trial and error in science as follows: First, the researcher encounters a problem, a puzzle she detects in reality, which inspires her to pursue inquiry. Second, she proposes a theoretical solution, a tentative theory that attempts to resolve the problem. Third, the researcher subjects her theory to attempts at elimination through critical discussion, including the use of experimental testing; that is, she searches for errors in her theory, where exactly it breaks down. Fourth, the errors of the theory she uncovers in the critical discussion open up new problems, and the entire cycle repeats itself. Research is dynamic and never finished. We can only come closer to truth but we can never be certain to have reached it.

How do researchers obtain their trials? Popper (1963) describes trials as conjectures:

> We are not passive receptors of sense data, but active organisms. [...] we can invent myths, stories, theories; because we have a thirst for explanation, an insatiable curiosity, a wish to know. Because by a great effort, by trying hard and making many mistakes, we may sometimes, if we are lucky, succeed in hitting upon a story, an explanation, which saves the phenomena.

Popper (1963) thus attributes our conjectures to an "irrational element" or a "creative intuition".

In school, or for that matter also in most universities, teachers and professors present their students with the "truth". For every question the students ask, they receive seemingly true feedback. The textbooks tell the students what is true, and in every examination they can end up further from or closer to this truth. In schools, the intellectual world is filled with illusions of platonic forms students just need to reach out for. In scientific reality, these made-up platonic forms quickly disappear, and researchers need to wrestle through the immense complexities of the actual knowledge base.

In their first years, PhD students tend to have great difficulties in finding original research questions. This difficulty is a manifestation of "Meno's paradox", as it appears in Plato's dialogue Meno (Plato, trans. 1892).

The paradox states that without also knowing the answer one cannot ask questions about a subject. Socrates formulates the paradox as follows:

> [...] a man cannot enquire either about that which he knows, or about that which he does not know; for if he knows, he has no need to enquire; and if not, he cannot; for he does not know the very subject about which he is to enquire.

Either you already know the answer, and thus have no need to ask questions, or, if you do not yet know the answer, you do not know what questions to ask. A solution to Meno's paradox is that no one is completely ignorant of everything. Everyone has at least some knowledge in some domains, which then serves as the basis to guide inquiry, by allowing assessing eventual progress as either correct or not, and from which one can work toward a correct answer. Hence, PhD students need to first dive into their subject and accumulate knowledge step-by-step; only over time they will start to notice anomalies about which they can ask questions. However, Meno's paradox can be frustrating, and the process of learning how to come up with original research questions is very hard.

The standard advice most researchers give to their PhD students is to read the existing literature and find holes in our understanding of a particular subject. Yet judgment about where to make valuable contributions that also extend the knowledge frontier is extremely difficult, as it requires an in-depth understanding of the direction in which the entire literature is moving. The closer a literature is to the frontier, the more difficult it becomes to know where it will head toward. If researchers interpret open problems wrongly, they will make less relevant contributions on the wrong side of the literature. And, of course, to make into the hall of fame of economics, solely applying existing methodologies will not suffice; one needs to invent a new method.

Moreover, applied economists always suffer from the fundamental curse of empirical research. We cannot tackle what is most interesting or relevant and instead have to settle with questions for which we have the necessary data and means for causal analysis. The easiest strategy for most applied economists is therefore to watch out for all sorts of natural experiments or quasi-experiments on literally any subject which is of interest to economics. If the available data allow the exploitation of either some form of randomization or of some type of exogenous structural break, such as a specific policy shock, the study will have good prospects to land in a solid academic journal.

Even though following the existing literature is most beneficial for scientific progress, it is a promising strategy only if the literature contains exclusively or predominantly true feedback. In contrast, if the majority of studies corresponds to false feedback, we need alternative windows to the economic world, since we cannot directly rely on the existing empirical evidence. We need other means to double-check our theories and even our empirical evidence itself; otherwise, we are prone to dive into a world detached from the actual economic developments.

Such alternative strategies to obtain valuable research ideas include i) using different media to follow important economic developments around the world; ii) gathering real-life experience to discover how the actual economic world looks like (e.g., Akerlof (1970), who closely observed the markets for used cars to grasp his concepts of asymmetric information); iii) reading a broad range of good books on any thinkable topic; iv) (informal) discussions with knowledgeable people with different backgrounds; v) relating insights from other disciplines to economics (e.g., much of behavioral economics is heavily influenced by psychology); vi) learning from patterns detected in the data (this sometimes very misleading practice will be discussed in the next chapters in great detail).

Coming up with inconsistent ideas is very easy. To generate valuable ideas, in contrast, requires not only imagination but also much analytic thinking. If you have many different ideas, you need to be able to sort out the best ones. Only a large amount of knowledge combined with rigorous analytic thinking enables evaluating whether a particular idea is useful or not. Just having an idea is trivial. Working out whether an idea indeed makes sense in light of all types of possible objections to the idea, on the other hand, is very hard. Only few ideas survive this filtering process.

Nonetheless, Popper (1963) is not so much concerned about how we get to our theoretical conjectures. Important is only that we continuously criticize our conjectures, meaning that we have to try to find instances that refute them. We can only find better theories if we point out the errors in our existing theories. Hence, to improve the theories we have formulated, we have to subject them to repeated instances of falsification. We need to identify the weaknesses of our current theories.

Popper (1972) thus argues that the starting points for our inquiries do not need to be secure; common sense notions are sufficient. The central aspect is to challenge and criticize these initial theoretical notions. Successful criticism allows us to modify and replace our initial attempts with more adequate theories. Consequently, Popper (1972) argues that the problem of knowledge is not secure foundations, as Descartes would demand it, but the growth of knowledge. The key is that we can make progress, that we can identify where we have been wrong and learn from our mistakes. The security needs not to lie in our theoretical but rather in our empirical insights. We require reliable empirical tests to know whether a theory is falsified or not; it is the criticism that needs to be secure.

Given reliable empirical tests, what is then the difference between falsification and verification of a hypothesis? Popper (1959) argues that falsification is the only epistemologically correct route in science; because of the problem of induction, we can never conclusively verify a hypothesis. Take the philosophy of science's commonly used example of the black swan problem. No matter how many white swans we will observe, we can never conclusively verify that all swans are white. In contrast, we have to observe only one black swan to conclusively falsify that all swans are white. To falsify only one case must be false, from which we can then deduce that the general statement about all the cases is false, too. Falsification relies on the "modus tollens", meaning that we can use deductive arguments to prove that an observation refutes an entire theoretical system. The arrow of the "modus tollens" is the only logical syllogism which shoots upward, without any use of induction (Lakatos 1970). In contrast, no amount of experience can conclusively verify inductive reasoning. Every argument of the validity of inductive reasoning faces the problem of infinite regress. If we use experience to argue that inductive reasoning is true, for example, that we have observed some empirical regularities in the past and that, therefore, empirical regularities exist, we are just building on an inductive principle of a higher order. Nonetheless, in Chapter 5 on the Duhem–Quine thesis, we will see that Popper's (1959) elegant approach of falsification suffers from a crucial problem, too, as empirical tests are not always reliable.

Moreover, despite the impossibility to conclusively verify a theory by gathering enough empirical evidence, we still need a criterion that indicates the degree of confidence we can have in a hypothesis that has passed many empirical tests. For example, consider knowledge about constructing a new airplane. Should we use empirically well-established theories, which have never been falsified, or brand new theories, which have also never been falsified? Theories need some kind of measure to indicate to what extent they are supported. Popper (1972) himself argued that theories are not verifiable in principle but that they can be corroborated, that is, what empirical tests they have withstood so far. Hence, we should try to assess how far a theory has been able to prove its fitness by standing up to tests. However, in all of this, a theory's survival until now will say nothing about its future survival.

Popper (1959) is in stark contrast to the method of Sherlock Holmes, who relies on existing facts, weights them against each other, and tries to wave everything into a reasonable whole. Sherlock Holmes considers all facts, even trivial ones, and only once all data are available, he proceeds to form a theory (Doyle 1914). However, while the method of Sherlock Holmes serves to create theories, it does not include the testing of theories. For this, Sherlock Holmes would need to make conjectures based on his theory and check whether they are in line with newly discovered facts. The method of Sherlock Holmes thus provides only preliminary theoretical insights, which have not yet passed empirical tests.

An important aspect of Popper's philosophy of science is his opposition to the introduction of ad-hoc hypotheses. He states as a methodological rule that scientists have to refrain from introducing arbitrary ad-hoc arguments to save their theories from falsification. Popper (1959) argues that there exist two exceptions in this. First, ad-hoc hypotheses are allowed if they increase the degree of falsifiability of the theory, that is, the theory now forbids more than before. Second, ad-hoc hypotheses are allowed if their influence can be isolated and empirically tested. If they pass such tests, they are acknowledged as valid ad-hoc hypotheses. Often the validity of ad-hoc hypotheses depends on how arbitrary they are. In fact, there exist many legitimate ad-hoc fixes in the history of science (e.g., the discovery of Neptune, which "saved" classical Newtonian mechanics from falsification).

Importantly, falsification in a null hypothesis setting does not require that the statistical estimates of an empirical test are close to zero coupled with small standard errors. Falsifications do not have to take the form of null effects. Researchers can also falsify a theory through providing evidence that contradicts its predictions. The prediction derived from the theory is thereby the null hypothesis, and, if the statistical estimates are significantly different from it, the prediction is false, and therefore also the theory. The difference between falsification and corroboration is not so much the applied setting, but rather the attitude of the researcher, whether he or she is actively trying to refute a theory.

Because falsification and corroboration are asymmetric, looking for narrow evidence to support a theory is problematic. The narrower the corroboratory evidence, the less relevant it becomes. For instance, a very specific operationalization of an experimental treatment provides only few corroboratory value, as the treatment may not provide corroboratory value under all other possible operationalizations. In contrast, to falsify a theory, already narrow evidence is sufficient. Even a very specific operationalization of an experimental operationalization can disprove the current state of a theory, as the theory breaks down in light of this fact. To corroborate a theory, only broad evidence is of value; we need a range of operationalizations of the experimental treatment to work out.

Moreover, Chalmers (2013) argues that falsification of a bold conjecture delivers only limited new insights. We do not gain much by refuting a hypothesis that seemed unlikely right from the outset. In contrast, falsification of a cautious conjecture can be of very high relevance. If we are able to refute a hypothesis that everyone has taken for granted, we can contribute a valuable insight to science. The reverse holds for corroboration of a bold conjecture, which can be of very high relevance, while the corroboration of a cautious conjecture adds only few additional values to the advance of science.

For instance, if a theory predicts that it will rain some days next April, and it indeed does so, no one will be much impressed by this fact. If, on the other hand, a theory predicts exactly how much it will rain each day next April, and it indeed does so, the theory will probably have substantial merit (Meehl 1978). The more such risky tests a theory has survived, the better corroborated it is.

Platt (1964) argues that we better pursue one crucial experiment than a hundred misguided experiments failing to address the central problem. In the natural sciences, such tests are sometimes feasible; for example, the detection of the Higgs boson is in the Large Hadron Collider is sufficient to establish it universally. In economics, in contrast, we lack crucial experiments that are large scale, relevant, and broadly applicable. There is no way we can change monetary policy in some randomly selected countries around the world and do this several times and in alternative ways. This inability to pursue crucial experiments is a central impediment for settling debates in economics. We are only seldom able to create the necessary setups for experiments that can decide the course we walk.

To sum up, according to Karl Popper, the target of science is to find evidence that falsifies the theory and not to find evidence that corroborates it. Researchers should make exact predictions that are dangerous for their theories and which would erase their entire fundament if false, and then test these empirically. However, in economics, almost all researchers are gathering evidence to confirm their theories. "We find evidence in line with X, Y, or Z" is the norm in almost all empirical studies.

In a science where criticism is alive, the problem that everyone searches for corroboration looms less large, as one side's corroboration is often another side's falsification. A researcher looking for evidence in line with his or her own hypothesis can contradict the hypothesis of other researchers. However, this contrast plays out well only if researchers directly confront each other. Unfortunately, upfront criticism of established theories is seldom welcome in economics; to present evidence in line with an alternative theory is a much more convenient path. The key is not to step on someone else's toes. Thus, even though science can only make progress if the trial and error results in commonly visible errors, they often hide from us, as no one has an incentive to find errors and openly expose them.

Popper (1963) argues that we can approach truth only through intense critical discussions. Yet we can never be certain to also have achieved truth even if some of our hypotheses do in fact correspond to it. Popper's critical discussions include what we have called repeated feedback. In the presence of false feedback, critical discussion is unlikely to lead any closer to truth; it may even lead to divergence from truth. Popper is very right that we cannot have certainty in our theories. However, in economics, we cannot have certainty in most of our critical discussions, too. Sometimes we may accidentally throw theories out of the window that are in fact true. Critical discussion is only fertile when based on repeated true feedback. Whether we should favor falsification over confirmation is thus subordinate in actual scientific practice. The emphasis needs first to be on whether we receive repeated true feedback. The next chapters will discuss why economics receives so much false feedback.

4 The garden of forking paths

4.1 Researcher degrees of freedom

The core thesis of this book is that the main driver behind false feedback in economics is the large discretionary room researchers have in specifying their empirical strategies. Simmons et al. (2011) call this discretionary room "researcher degrees of freedom", which they define as the "flexibility in data collection, analysis, and reporting". Researcher degrees of freedom result from an ambiguity in making the right choices to obtain a valid empirical strategy. Every empirical strategy entails numerous different and important decisions about how to proceed. They determine which way the entire enterprise goes and can be very difficult to evaluate correctly. Often the researchers could rightfully have made many alternative series of decisions. This book argues that the more researcher degrees of freedom a given empirical study entails, the higher the likelihood is that the study produces false feedback.

Gelman and Loken (2013) describe the variety of options researchers have when making their decisions for an empirical strategy as a "garden of forking paths". The "garden of forking path" is a short story by the Argentinian writer Jorge Luis Borges (1941)[1]. Gelman and Loken (2013) use it to express the idea of a simultaneous presence of a large number of alternative ways to analyze the data. Researchers choose a particular series of methodological decisions that results in a corresponding statistical finding. Yet there would also have existed the possibility of having chosen very different series of decisions, leading to always different statistical findings. Of all the potential series of decisions to carry out empirical strategy, only one is realized, while all others remain hidden.

Inspired by Gelman and Loken (2013), I will define the sum of all the different options a researcher has to build his or her empirical strategy as the *garden of forking paths*. Importantly, and in contrast to Gelman and Loken (2013), this chapter of the book will exclusively focus on whether a given series of decisions about the empirical strategy is adequate or not independent of concerns of statistical noise. That is, it abstracts from a large influence of sample variation and assumes that a given series of methodological decisions leads to relatively similar statistical findings over alternative datasets, such as, for instance, in the case of large samples, which are in general much less affected by statistical noise than smaller samples. Of course, statistical noise can be a huge contributor to false feedback, too, even in large samples. P-values would provide us with a tool to quantify the extent of statistical noise. However, to be valid, p-values require that all of the assumptions of the statistical model hold up. That is, p-values demand that we have made the right choices along our ways through the garden of forking paths. Before we can discuss issues surrounding p-values, we need to know how to proceed such that the statistical model becomes true, which turns out to be very difficult. In every research setup, different researchers tend to walk along sometimes very different paths, as they choose different combinations from the vast universe of available researcher degrees freedom. They walk along the same paths only by accident, thereby creating large variation in the obtained feedback.

The number of available researcher degrees of freedom can be excessively large. To illustrate, Table 4.1 shows examples of researcher degrees of freedom at the level of the data analysis in a typical observational study in economics. Table 4.1 is certainly not exhaustive. These are only the most obvious researcher degrees of freedom, which regularly appear in the data analysis stage of most empirical study. Many more hide in the idiosyncrasies of the respective studies, especially in the data collecting, processing, and cleaning stages. Some of these researcher degrees of freedom have a large impact, others have only a small impact. Important is that they enter multiplicatively and jointly create a huge matrix of available researcher degrees of freedom. Together they define the discretionary room researchers have in their empirical analyses. Because they enter multiplicatively, the number of potential ways through the garden of forking paths is gigantic. If we assume only three possibilities for each of the 18 researcher degrees of freedoms in Table 4.1, we get a total of $3^{18} = 387{,}420{,}489$ different forking paths, that is, researchers can choose one or several ways out of these millions of alternative ways.

Of course, researchers are seldom entirely free in all of their choices in the vast garden of forking paths. If they set out to test a well-specified theory, the theory will dictate certain aspects of the empirical strategy, meaning that the room of available researcher degrees of freedom shrinks. In contrast, if they test a set of theoretically more isolated hypotheses, the room of available researcher degrees of freedom is very large. We will discuss the crucial connection between both theory and empirical strategy in Section 6.4. Here we assume that researchers set out to test more isolated hypotheses *not* backed up by a precise theory, giving substantial room to researchers, as this approach has become more common in applied economics over time (see, e.g., Biddle and Hamermesh 2017).

The garden of forking paths is not just a problem for simple multiple correlational studies but is as relevant for well-identified, causality-oriented

Table 4.1 Examples of researcher degrees of freedom in the data analysis stage

Dataset	Sample	Time dimension (cross-section, time series, panel)
Outcome variable	Explanatory variables	Leads or lags of variables
Measurement of variables	Coding of variables (e.g., continuous, binary, ordinal, ratio, normalized, index)	Handling of missing values
Level of analysis (e.g., individuals, households, firms, regions, countries)	What kind of fixed effects (e.g., individual, group, time, group × time) and how detailed	Focus on subset of data with certain characteristics (e.g., specific groups or periods)
Eligibility for and timing of treatment	functional form (e.g., linear, quadratic, exponential, polynomial, interaction term)	Handling of extreme observations (e.g., retain, winsorize, truncate, scale)
Estimation method (e.g., OLS/GLS/NLS, (Q) ML, matching, GMM, ML methods)	Settings of the chosen estimation method	Standard errors (e.g., normal, robust, cluster, bootstrap)

research designs such as instrumental variable analysis, difference-in-differences, regression discontinuity, or randomized controlled trials. In any of these research designs, the researcher encounters countless variations of different researcher degrees of freedom. However, most causal research designs do put some constraints on the specification of the statistical model and thus reduce the space of available choices in the garden of forking paths somewhat. A difference-in-differences design, for example, has to be modeled in specific ways. Every causal research design forbids at least some specification choices, as they would make the estimated treatment effects endogenous again (these are usually context dependent though). Nonetheless, while causal research designs do dictate certain choices in the garden of forking paths, they remain silent about the large majority of all other choices. Unfortunately, many of these remaining researcher degrees of freedom have no less impact on results. Thus, while causal research designs invalidate certain specification choices of the statistical model, they do not constrain the choices within the set of researcher degrees of freedom that are still available, and the latter generally remain very numerous.

The focus on research designs has caused a shift away from how to choose the true econometric model in a given context toward how to choose the context to make a given econometric model come true. The search for exogenous sources of variation has made the use of complex econometric methods superfluous. The econometric methods used in applied economics are thus relatively simple nowadays. Experiments, for instance, may not go beyond a simple comparison of means. However, research designs have also introduced new researcher degrees of freedom, namely, all those steps that lead within a given empirical strategy from the raw data toward the applied econometric model. Researchers do not just anymore take up some publicly available dataset and try to fit an econometric model on it; they rather collect, clean, and process their own data, with all the additional forking paths coming along with this. And many of these choices of researcher degrees of freedom lying between the collection of raw data and the formulation of the applied model can cause huge differences.

Moreover, a very clean natural experiment does not leave less researcher degrees of freedom than a less clean natural experiment. The degree of exogeneity in an identification strategy does not affect the general availability of researcher degrees of freedom that this particular type of identification strategy offers. Whether the allocation mechanism of the treatment is random or not does not affect how the treatment will be analyzed subsequently, with all the many intermediate steps.

The actual number of available researcher degrees of freedom certainly also depends on the context within which the study takes place. Some contexts allow many researcher degrees of freedom, others only few. The crucial aspect is that from the outside it is generally difficult to judge how many researcher degrees of freedom the authors of the study had available in their respective context.

Importantly, even though they may be hard or even impossible to pin down, the researcher degrees of freedom at a given forking path are seldom fully interchangeable. Researchers may not be able to verify which choice of researcher degrees of freedom is the correct one, but this does not make all of the available options equally true. Most of the time, only a subset of choices or even only one particular choice out of all the available researcher degrees of freedom is correct, meaning that only they render the statistical model true.

Researchers therefore face uncertainty about the adequacy of their available choices in the garden of forking paths. They often lack the information necessary to decide which of the available researcher degrees of freedom are the right way to go. They *think* that all of the available choices are equally true, while in reality they are not. The researchers have too often simply no means to access the information that would allow making a correct evaluation of all the available researcher degrees of freedom. This inevitable ignorance of sometimes crucial idiosyncrasies can give rise to choices that lead far away from the true statistical model.

If researchers know only little about a subject, every possible option seems equally true to them. They cannot think of any reasons why one of them should be false, as they lack the necessary information to arrive at these judgments. Given they perceive all available options as equally true, they will choose arbitrarily, as they will deem their choices as inconsequential.

Yet uncertainty at a given forking path means that one path is correct and one or several other paths are not, but in our perspective as detached researchers we have no way of knowing the true path. More information can help here the researchers to come to a better decision. By digging up further details, they can discover that one of the available degrees of freedom is more appropriate than others. This pursuit always reaches a limit though, and whether researchers will then choose this way or that way depends heavily on their respective information set.

Sometimes, however, none of the available options at a given forking path are fully adequate, and researchers necessarily produce false feedback, irrespective of their choices. If all the options at a given forking are at the same time equally correct and incorrect, they create a special set of researcher degrees of freedom, which cannot be dissolved by gathering additional information. These particular instances, causing wide variation in feedback, are the topic of the next chapter.

4.2 Equipollence

False feedback arises when researchers choose a wrong way through the garden of forking paths. The chosen series of forking paths results in a statistical model that does not adequately represent reality, and the formulated model violates one or several of its assumptions. Whereas every economist is aware of how crucial assumptions are for the results in a theoretical model, satisfying assumptions is in fact even more important in statistical models. The main purpose of economic theory is to generate insights into the working of the economy. Theorists are less interested in portraying reality exactly as it is but how things play out in producing certain outcomes. Because the insight into economic mechanisms occupies center stage, it is less relevant whether all of the model's assumptions are exactly met. They may even be the key to the insights themselves. In contrast, in empirical research, we want to get true descriptions of how the world really is. We therefore have to map economic reality as closely as possible. If, however, we choose a wrong way through the garden of forking paths, we will deviate from an exact representation of reality, and the applied estimations produce false feedback.

The applied statistical model defines how exactly researchers see the world. If the world is different from the proposed model, we will obtain false feedback. Unfortunately, those ways through the garden of forking paths that indeed meet all assumptions of the statistical model are notoriously difficult to get at. Consider, for example, the case of the very frequently used OLS estimator. OLS forces all of the explanatory variables to be orthogonal to the residuals. This is a mathematical property of the OLS estimator. The error terms, in contrast, are usually not orthogonal to the explanatory variables; they become orthogonal only if the specified statistical model is true. OLS does not know whether the orthogonality condition is indeed satisfied, but it nonetheless calculates results as such. It has no way of knowing whether in reality the orthogonality condition is violated or not. OLS runs its neat program of orthogonal residuals irrespective of how things in fact are. Applying OLS in such a case thus forces an inappropriate modeling structure on the data and produces false feedback. The researchers think that their estimated statistical model is true albeit the true statistical model can be very different.

Often there is no unambiguously true path through the garden of forking paths, even if researchers had all the information necessary. The decisions for implementing an empirical strategy researchers make are generally more or less correct, but seldom fully so. Sometimes they can make no sensible decision at all, meaning that the decision in favor of a given aspect of the setup is no more correct than incorrect. This can happen when there are insufficient grounds to make an appropriate decision, and the judgments about how to proceed in the research project end up at an impasse.

Often you are certain initially that a given decision is the correct one. However, if you start digging deeper into the subject, you will start discovering aspects that render things much more complicated and that actually alternative decisions leading into different directions would be adequate options as well. Ideally, you can weigh all options, and then make an informed conclusion in favor of a decision holding up to different objections. Sometimes, though, you cannot possibly make a correct decision and remain stuck in light of the contrasting arguments for the alternative options.

There are almost always some reasons speaking in favor of a given choice and other reasons speaking against it. A particular choice can be appropriate on some dimensions, while at the same time it is inappropriate on other dimensions. An illustrative example for such a conflict is the choice between different measures of abstract concepts, which can always shed light on some aspects of the concept while neglecting others. For instance, the various existing indicators for democracy differ strongly in the content they measure. Each indicator captures some aspects of democracy at the cost of omitting other aspects. Even abstract concepts that are of a quantitative nature can be difficult to capture. For instance, there is an entire literature discussing how to best measure inflation, with each approach having its own strengths and weaknesses (see, e.g., Reiss 2008).

Impasses emerge because the reasons that speak for or against a given choice are vague. For example, we might have several reasons that speak in favor of a given choice and only a single reason that speaks against it, but this one single reason might weigh heavily. Because we can hardly quantify and therefore directly compare the different reasons, it becomes impossible to make a reliable statement about which set of reasons dominates.

Consider the following hypothetical examples of choices for an appropriate statistical model where the researchers end up at an impasse: i) a control variable partials out undesired variance in the association between the dependent variable and the right-hand side variables, while it simultaneously also partials out desired variance. ii) Tackling one source of endogeneity requires an estimation strategy that makes it impossible to also tackle another important source of endogeneity. iii) Applying a linear model lacks the flexibility to catch more complex patterns, while a nonlinear model is harder to interpret and more prone to overfitting. iv) A number of outliers are different from all other observations because of some particular reasons, but nevertheless bear important resemblances to them, and eliminating the outliers strongly affects results. v) The imputation of missing values for a given variable maintains observations for other explanatory variables, which increases their estimated precision, yet faces the problem of a repetition of the same informational content for the variable itself.

The Pyrrhonian Skeptic Sextus Empiricus (about 200 CE) termed the situation when the arguments for a cause have no more weight than the arguments against it "equipollence". The term equipollence means literally "to be equal of force". Sextus Empiricus defined it as "equality in respect to probability and improbability, to indicate that none of the conflicting judgements takes precedence of any other as being more probable". In his work "The outlines of Pyrrhonism" (Sextus Empiricus, trans. 1990) he described the so-called skeptic "modes", which are tools for argumentation the skeptic uses in his investigation. For example, the mode based on regress ad infinitum: no argument can rely on a proof, since this proof will require itself a further proof, and so on ad infinitum. The modes are tools so powerful that the skeptic naturally ends up at equipollence. Every investigation, every thorough inquiry of a subject, is destined to result in an impasse. The skeptic then has no other option than to suspend judgment, which, counterintuitively, will not disturb him but provide him with quietude, a mind free of perturbation. This in turn allows him to live a life in line with only inevitable things, such as the passions, and act accordingly. Because every investigation will result in a balance of reasons speaking for or against a particular cause, where both sides of the debate turn out equally persuasive or unpersuasive, suspension of judgment is the obvious consequence. In contrast, if researchers end up at an instant of equipollence, they will not simply suspend judgment and relax, but rather break the impasse by making some (arbitrary) decision in favor of or against one of the available options.

Importantly, equipollence does not emerge at every forking path. To the contrary, most decisions between the alternative options available to the researcher will be relatively clear. Yet in every research project, instances of equipollence will open up at along the chosen way through the garden of forking paths. Thus, while equipollence is not the norm, it will occur at specific decisions.

Equipollence is especially salient if two methodological aims are in conflict with each other. Choice X could tackle one important problem, whereas choice Y could tackle another important problem, but, since the two choices remain mutually exclusive, researchers can opt for only one of them; they cannot possibly address both problems simultaneously. Equipollence is also common if a choice corresponds to the standard textbook solution adequate in the general situation "X", but the specific context of situation "x" provides good reasons for an alternative solution, while neither of the two solutions is fully adequate. In such cases, equipollence depends heavily on the situation under investigation. Sometimes a correct choice is possible, other times it is not easily feasible.

Equipollence becomes very explicit if you read the research of others. Every time you ask yourself at a particular decision in the study why the authors proceeded this particular, only partly valid way, and not another, also only partly valid way, you have hit on a potential instance of equipollence. The reasons the authors give for their decision contrast with the reasons you yourself have in mind. In fact, at a given forking path, researchers usually have many different options available, like, for example, on which level to cluster standard errors, and do not face a simple choice of "either this way or that". In these cases, equipollence emerges if the available options are equally true or false, that is, all of them are somewhat correct but still problematic in certain ways, such that none of the options stands out among all the others. For instance, discussing the use of weights in regression models, Angrist and Pischke (2008) acknowledge:

> Few things are as confusing to applied researchers as the role of sample weights. Even now, 20 years post-Ph.D., we read the section of the Stata manual on weighting with some dismay. Weights can be used in a number of ways, and how they are used may well matter for your results. Regrettably, however, the case for or against weighting is often less than clear-cut, as are the specifics of how the weights should be programmed.

It is the equipollence inherent in the decisions creating this impasse.

This section frames equipollence as objective. The nature of empirical research is to be confronted with equipollence at specific forking paths such that no objectively correct decision can be made. Every researcher would face the same trade-offs at the same forking paths such that equipollence becomes inevitable. The result is large variation in the obtained empirical feedback between different researchers. However, equipollence can also be subjective. Different researchers perceive different forking paths as equally valid options. If this is the case, the review process may help out, such that author and reviewers can converge toward at most the objective instances of equipollence.

Even in the more common case of an absence of equipollence, that is, the balance of the arguments is in favor of one side, such as mostly right and somewhat wrong, the decision in favor of the more persuasive side will still be partly false. Any methodological choice constrains the statistical model by leaving out at least some aspect of reality and thus contributes to the generation of false feedback. Decisions in the empirical setup of a study contribute to true feedback only if they are unambiguously correct, which, unfortunately, is a rather rare case. We are often forced to choose one particular way even though it is only mostly right and still somewhat wrong.

To make meaningful statements, we have to mold the complexity of economic reality into a simplified empirical setup. We cannot have both sides of each trade-off simultaneously; we are forced to settle with only one side. Methodological choices thus inevitably distort the true state of things, which can only be represented up to some extent, giving rise to vagueness in empirical estimates. The result is an empirical setup producing deviations from true feedback that are hard to predict.

The adequacy of many decisions in the garden of forking paths is consequently hard to pin down. Instances of equipollence are not probabilistically true or false. They are vague, that is, they are equally true and false, just like some undefined color that falls in between the categories we commonly refer to. For instance, suppose you have 50 bottles of wine and 50 bottles of water. If you do not have information on which bottle contains wine and which contains water, you face a probability of 0.5 to pick a bottle of wine and a probability of 0.5 to pick a bottle of water. However, after having randomly chosen a bottle, it contains either wine or water. In contrast, suppose you have 100 bottles that all contain 50% wine and 50% water. There is no lack of knowledge with respect to the content of the bottles, you know that each bottle is a perfect mixture of wine and water, irrespective of which bottle you pick. The bottles fall outside our common categories. Some decisions in the garden of forking paths are in this same manner equally true and false, that is, they represent instances of equipollence.

Russell (1923) argues that language is vague, not the objects we refer to. Vagueness arises because our applied concepts do not represent reality accurately. Russell (1956) states that "Everything is vague to a degree you do not realize till you have tried to make it precise". One only needs to have a closer look to understand how vague things really are. To combat the problem of vagueness, we would need better theories, which can dissect what is vague and divide it into finer parts until the required level of precision. Russell (1923) states that "[...] there is less vagueness in the near appearance than in the distant one. There is still less vagueness about the appearance under the microscope". Albeit vagueness is omnipresent, we can make things more precise by looking closer. Hence, to dissolve instances of equipollence, or similar forms of misrepresentation, we would more precise theories.

4.3 Silent steps

We have not yet discussed the numerous researcher degrees of freedom present in the preparation of the raw data that every empirical strategy requires. They are a special form of researcher degrees of freedom because they are much less salient and often remain hidden to the eye of readers of the published study. I thus call this special set of researcher degrees of freedom "silent steps". They not only encompass the data processing and cleaning stages but also the data collection stage, that is, the setup and the corresponding execution of the entire study. In general, the larger and more complex a research project, the more silent steps it will incorporate along its way up to the final estimations.

To obtain an approximate idea of how many silent steps the data cleaning and processing stages of a given study involve, we can look at the number of transformations researchers perform on the raw data. To this end, we can simply count the number of code lines used to transform the raw data such that we arrive at the final dataset ready for the data analysis stage. Of course, the totality of these code lines will only represent a lower boundary, as many of the applied transformations on the raw data will offer a great variety of options about how to proceed, multiplying the potential number of silent steps by orders of magnitudes. As a general rule, the more data transformations and thus the more silent steps it requires until the raw data are ready for running the data analysis, the less likely it becomes that an independent researcher without access to all the coding files can replicate it.

The published study of course documents the outline of every empirical strategy but often leaves out silent steps that are nonetheless crucial for the obtained results and, at the same time, are far from obvious to other researchers. Transformations of raw data that seem rather innocent at first can sometimes have a sizeable influence on results, and it is hardly possible for the reader to judge whether an alternative processing and cleaning of the raw data would have led to different results. The target of the scientific edifice is to produce results that satisfy intersubjective objectivity, meaning that other researchers can independently verify and reproduce the empirical evidence. The existence of numerous silent steps in the preparation of the raw data thus causes substantial trouble, because a lot of potentially relevant information about the empirical strategy remains absent.

Every student I worked with who wanted to replicate a published study to afterward build on its results ran into a series of difficulties, even though the students used the very same data and tried to apply the very same empirical strategy as outlined in the published study. The results were sometimes similar but each time still rather far away from the results actually reported in the published study. The more complicated the applied method was, the worse it got. The large number of silent steps involved made it impossible to reconstruct the complete empirical strategy.

To replicate a study only based on the published manuscript, that is, without access to the coding files of the original authors, can give interesting insights into the influence of all the silent steps involved in the study, because one gets true feedback whether one has walked along the same path as the original authors. If the estimation results differ, the chosen path is clearly not same. If the estimation results match, the path is not said to be exactly same, but at least likely to be very similar. The process of independent replication gives a good impression of how many silent steps a given empirical study involves. In general, the more trials a researcher needs to match the results of a given study, the higher the likelihood that the study contains a large number of silent steps. An exact replication of even just the most important findings of a study can prove very difficult without access to all original coding files; just a few different choices of the silent steps can complicate it enormously.

Even simple descriptive information can be difficult to replicate. Descriptive statistics are the fundament to every reasoned discussion. They often serve as the starting point for a series of arguments and, if important enough, can sometimes debunk entire theories (given that they are not just ignored, of course). One might think that calculating descriptive statistics should be rather straightforward and that silent steps should have little to no room here. This is not always the case though. Putting together, descriptive statistics opens up not only questions about how to handle missing values, strange entries, or errors in the data, but also how to deal with the applied sampling methods, differences across time and space, and, most important, how to best convey the relevant information.

Take, for example, the discussions about the adequacy of the descriptive statistics in Thomas Piketty's popular book "Capital in the 21st century". Piketty's book has initially been commended from all sides for its high-quality statistical work (Gilles 2014). However, a team from the Financial Times claims to have found "mistakes and unexplained entries" in Piketty's spreadsheets (Gilles 2014). They write that after they "cleaned up and simplified the data, the European numbers do not show any tendency toward rising wealth inequality after 1970" (Gilles 2014). Hence, even in statistical work concerning descriptive statistics, silent steps can be extremely relevant, irrespective of the perceived quality of the work. Redoing silent steps can flip the conclusions derived from them.

If researchers calculate only a few disconnected descriptive statistics, most problems inherent to the data will remain hidden; they can apply some ad-hoc rules and have thus no way of realizing that they may have taken one or several suboptimal forking paths. If, however, they calculate a whole series of interrelated descriptive statistics from the data, the problems will start to show up, because these statistics have to be mutually consistent with each other. Only tedious double-checking of all the descriptive statistics allows discovering the errors responsible for such discrepancies.

The institution I worked at had regularly published policy reports with many descriptive statistics. Every time other researchers, who did not have access to our coding files, tried to replicate some of these descriptive statistics from our data, they obtained, without exception, always somewhat different results, even though we gave them all the information about the respective definitions and methods. And neither we nor they had any incentive to misrepresent the data. The silent steps, which were part of calculating even these simple descriptive statistics, made it impossible for them to reconstruct the exact numbers. The replications always involved a slightly different, though no less valid, set of silent steps. A doctoral student and I once spent an entire day trying to replicate some descriptive statistics from a 20-year-old report. We had access to the exact same, fully prepared dataset, but we did not have access to the coding files they had used back then. In the end, we were so frustrated that we gave up. We sometimes came close, but we never hit the exact same numbers. So even in the simple case of constructing a set of simple descriptive statistics, where it should be straightforward to repeatedly obtain the same outcome, silent steps can lead to marked differences in results.

The inability to reproduce results is not unique to economics. Baker (2016) surveyed 1576 researchers from different fields. She finds that more than 70% of scientists have tried and failed to reproduce other researchers' experiments, and more than 50% have tried and failed to reproduce their own experiments. This pattern remains remarkably stable over numerous scientific fields: chemistry, biology, physics and engineering, medicine, earth environment, and "other" (Baker 2016).

Data cleaning is a science all by itself, which we learn almost nothing about. Everyone is self-taught and follows his or her own rules about how to best deal with the imperfections present in each dataset. This informality massively increases arbitrariness in decisions regarding all silent steps.

The closer you look at the data, the worse it gets. If you just calculate some aggregated statistics, without inspecting individual entries in more detail, everything looks fine. Once you start to dissect the data and compare various entries with each other, you start to notice all kinds of problems.

In addition to ambiguities about how to proceed correctly, large numbers of silent steps also increase the probability that one commits an error. While some decisions about particular silent steps would in fact be unambiguous, researchers can simply oversee them, reason wrongly, or make coding errors. This problem is hard to quantify; we can only conjecture that the larger the number of silent steps in a study, the higher the likelihood that researchers will commit at least some errors.

Experiments usually imply a very simple identification strategy of comparing treatment groups to control groups, where a simple test of a difference in means may already suffice. However, researchers can embark on false ways through the garden of forking paths in experiments, too. Whereas in experiments researchers face fewer problems in formulating the correct model specification, they suffer from difficulties in correctly setting up and executing the experiment. The way an experiment is carried out can strongly affect findings. Experiments do not just have silent steps in the cleaning and processing of the data but already in the data generating stage itself. Common problems when carrying out an experiment are, for instance, inadequate randomization, noncompliance, or incomplete blinding, which can all cause bias to the obtained estimates. Hence, while in experiments researchers can worry less about potential confounders, they have to worry more about all kinds of technical aspects that might invalidate the experiment right from the outset. In general, the more complex the setup of an experiment, the larger the danger that researchers take some wrong turns along the numerous possible ways to carry out the experiment. Experiments are thus less affected by variation in visible researcher degrees of freedom but mostly by variation in silent steps in the data collection stage, which are those more hidden researcher degrees of freedom in setting up and executing the experiment.

Bédécarrats et al. (2019) conduct a reanalysis of Crépon et al. (2015), which they consider a "flagship RCT". They show how strongly findings can vary when correcting and altering specific silent steps in reasonable ways. The large number of code lines in Crépon et al. (2015) make the study vulnerable to such variation. The cleaning and processing from the raw data to the final dataset takes over 4000 code lines, while the analysis takes another 2000 code lines. It is almost a necessity that with these many code lines alternative ways to handle the data will open up, even when neglecting critical choices in the data collecting stage. Whereas RCT generally face less researcher degrees of freedom in the data analysis stage, their generally more complex experimental setups carry along much more silent steps, not only in the data collection stage but also in the data processing and cleaning stages.

Observational studies face the same problem when they are based on datasets collected through researchers (via, e.g., web crawlers or archive searches). In such cases, the silent steps are extremely numerous, as researchers can decide about what kind of information to include, how to include it, what to omit, etc., where most of these decisions remain invisible to other researchers.

4.4 Variation in feedback

In every empirical strategy, most researcher degrees of freedom will remain unverifiable. Because they do not have good reasons for their choices of researcher degrees of freedom, different researchers will naturally choose different ways through the garden of forking paths. They will coincide in their judgments about which researcher degrees of freedom to choose only by chance. Different researchers will thus obtain different statistical findings, even if they proceed as truthful as possible. Because researcher degrees of freedom are often interlinked, it can matter a lot whether a researcher decides "left" or "right" at a given forking path. Every applied researcher knows that changing one particular degree of freedom can cause a small difference in results under one state of all other degrees of freedom and a large difference under an alternative state of all other degrees of freedom. A number of seemingly minor decisions about how to handle researcher degrees of freedom may thus lead researchers to encounter large differences in the obtained findings. The very nature of researcher degrees of freedom inhibits knowledge about which of these ways through the garden of forking paths is more adequate. Consequently, we will observe potentially large variation in false feedback without being able to judge whether one of the pursued paths better approaches true feedback than others.

Whereas different researcher degrees of freedom may be equally unverifiable, they are not all equally true. Some researcher degrees of freedom, even though we may not know it, will be more adequate than others. It can thus matter a lot how researchers choose their ways through the garden of forking paths. While the ways they choose may seem equally adequate, most often they are not.

A series of decisions toward the final empirical strategy can also exhibit substantial path dependency. Because many decisions in the garden of forking paths depend on each other, they can change their mutual adequacy. That is to say different choices in the garden of forking paths can alter the truth-falsity ratio of other choices. Only a subset of decisions remains the same irrespective of how all other decisions are made. Hence, if researchers start out with certain set of decisions, it will likely influence many of their later decisions. If they had started out differently, they would in many instances have chosen otherwise later on. This can also imply that when researchers choose at one forking path, some researcher degrees of freedom vanish, while new ones emerge. The true way through the garden of forking paths constantly dodges and moves around, not unlike if you squeeze a balloon.

Nonetheless, some among the numerous alternative series of decisions in the garden of forking paths may approach true feedback best. To address this problem of large potentiality, we need to show all relevant ways through the garden of forking paths in a highly aggregated manner, and then decide which of them are likely to be most adequate. The studies of Simonsohn et al. (2020) and Steegen et al. (2016) move into this direction; researchers would need to show the entirety of possibly valid ways though the garden of forking paths, constituting the multiverse of possibilities (see Section 14.4).

Even if a certain decision in the garden of forking path is more appropriate than the available alternatives, at least some researchers will always disagree about it. Every researcher has experienced different problems of different intensity in his or her previous work. Such past experience can strongly shape the respective researchers' beliefs about which decision is most appropriate. For example, one researcher may have observed numerous instances of severe sample selection. He or she will then naturally be inclined to stress concerns of sample selection and subordinate most other potential decisions to this particular concern. This implies that different researchers can interpret the exact same situation in quite different ways and subsequently embark on different forking paths, too. Hence, even if a certain way through the garden of forking paths approaches true feedback best, a diverse experience of past problems among researchers can cause substantial variation in the expected feedback.

In contrast to the overly rational perspective we took so far, which tackled every decision according to its circumstances, the research community has many conventions about how certain statistical decisions should be made. Because of such agreements about how to "correctly" proceed at a given forking path, some researchers tend to forget that most of their decisions are in fact trade-offs and, subsequently, become blind to false feedback. Whether conventions can indeed foster obtaining true feedback remains an open question. Whereas they reduce inter-researcher variation in statistical choices, they can also lead researchers into the wrong direction. We do not receive true feedback about whether a given statistical choice is indeed appropriate or not. Monte Carlo simulations are an exception here, but they often take part in an artificial environment that seldom corresponds to the actual situation under investigation. Conventions are also seldom an appropriate response to the unique properties of specific situations; while a convention about a certain statistical choice may be adequate in the majority of all cases, it can be completely inadequate in all the remaining cases.

The crucial difference here to practical tasks like engineering is that practitioners get true feedback about whether the separate physical elements constituting their work object also do their job accordingly. Researchers, in contrast, are very often blind to whether their chosen methodological elements are adequate or not. Over time, they may even get more and more certain of actually false choices, especially if other researchers regularly commit the same mistaken choices.

Silberzahn and Uhlmann (2015) and Silberzahn et al. (2018) investigate a setting where the variation in empirical estimates resulting from different statistical choices becomes very evident. They rely on a crowdsourcing initiative with 29 different teams of researchers. The authors gave each of the 29 teams the same large dataset and instructed them to answer the exact same research question: whether football referees are more likely to give red cards to players with dark skin than to players with light skin. The 29 teams were free to make their own decisions about how to best analyze the data. Even though the teams reviewed each other's statistical approaches, they chose a "wide array of analytical techniques, and obtained highly varied results" (Silberzahn and Uhlmann 2015). The ensuing discussion between the 29 teams did not lead to consensus on a single best approach, too. Importantly, the initial beliefs of the researchers about the subject, their statistical expertise, and the mutually rated quality of their different approaches could not explain the high variability in both the methodological choices and empirical results (Silberzahn et al. 2018). Hence, even within such a narrow research setup, many decisions about what would in fact be the correct way to pursue could not be decided by rational argumentation.

In practice, the variation that the numerous possible choices of researcher degrees of freedom inflict on the estimated effects combine with the variation that originates in the statistical noise of the respective sample. Together these two sources of variation amplify each other, causing even larger variation in the obtained estimates.

I argue that the size of the garden of forking paths has a negative effect on the growth of knowledge in a scientific field. In particular, I argue that the growth of knowledge is a negative function of the variation in feedback the respective empirical methods produce. To illustrate this point, consider the following very simple mathematical model: Δ(knowledge) = alpha + f(var(error|X)) with f(0)=0 and f'()<0, where "alpha" is a positive constant implying that in the case of true feedback there is positive growth of knowledge. In words, the more researcher degrees of freedom there are in the empirical methods in a given scientific field, the less reliable its empirical studies and thus the slower the growth of knowledge will be. Note that this simple mathematical model implies that if there is a sufficiently high variance of the empirical feedback, the growth of knowledge may even turn negative.

We are particularly likely to observe false feedback if effects are i) small, ii) variable, and iii) nosily measured (Gelman 2018). In such a case, minor deviations from the true path through the garden of forking paths will easily swamp the true effects and lead to false feedback. In contrast, we are more likely to observe true feedback if effects are i) large, ii) stable, and iii) precisely measured. Such effects are likely to show up irrespective of the ways taken through the garden of forking paths.

The broad variation in results also does not average out over all the different studies, since they are explicitly designed to be sufficiently different from each other and are therefore not directly comparable. The publishing system requires that new studies distinguish themselves from all previous studies; researchers need to make novel contributions to the literature. Thus, instead of providing alternative estimates of how to walk along the garden of forking paths, researchers have to enter new gardens of forking paths; they have to deliberately go around the content of previous studies. Yet to obtain reliable empirical evidence, we would need alternative shots at the very same hypotheses, with these shots designed to be comparable to each other. Instead, researchers are forced to investigate all sorts of variations around the content of previous studies. This is visible everywhere in the literature; just run a search for a specific economic hypothesis. You will find huge variation in the investigated hypotheses applied to an equally huge variation in the investigated contexts, but very seldom you will find a range of shots at the very same hypothesis that are explicitly designed to be comparable, even if you are after the most basic economic insights. We thus hardly know whether the differences between two empirical findings originate in variation in the ways the researchers have taken through their respective gardens of forking paths, or whether they lie in discrepancies in the hypotheses and contexts of studies. Before we can investigate variation in our hypotheses, we have to make sure that what we have shown so far indeed corresponds to approximately true feedback. Otherwise, we cannot hope to make much progress. If new contributions are not based on solid previous contributions, the strive for novelty will slow down progress and only let us end up in one dead end after the other.

Hubbard and Lindsay (2013a, 2013b) and Hubbard (2015) call out the current paradigm focusing on single works that allegedly constitute "original" research. Hubbard (2015) cites Nelder (1986), who termed it in his presidential address to the Royal Statistical Society as "the cult of the isolated study". Hubbard and Lindsay (2013a) argue that currently a single study is seen as satisfactorily addressing its respective research question, and that, after having it settled, researchers quickly move on to another piece of "original" research. Hubbard (2015) argues that what should constitute only the first step in establishing a specific result is too often regarded as the last word. The "cult of the isolated study" results in "a literature composed chiefly of fragmented, one-off results whose contributions to knowledge are of the most speculative kind" (Hubbard 2015). To overcome this situation, Hubbard and Lindsay (2013a, 2013b) and Hubbard (2015) recommend a shift away from a paradigm of "significant difference" toward a new paradigm of "significant sameness". Instead of explicitly differentiating themselves from previous studies, researchers should try collectively to uncover empirical regularities in their studies. Over time, these studies would then allow for convergence toward a set of stable facts, upon which Hubbard (2015) argues we can then, through inductive inference, build our theories.

Note

1 "The Garden of Forking Paths is a picture, incomplete yet not false, of the universe such as Ts'ui Pen conceived it to be. Differing from Newton and Schopenhauer, your ancestor did not think of time as absolute and uniform. He believed in an infinite series of times, in a dizzily growing, ever spreading network of diverging, converging, and parallel times. This web of time – the strands of which approach one another, bifurcate, intersect, or ignore each other through the centuries – embraces every possibility. We do not exist in most of them. In some you exist and not I, while in others I do, and you do not, and in yet others both of us exist. In this one, in which chance has favored me, you have come to my gate. In another, you, crossing the garden, have found me dead. In yet another, I say these very same words, but am an error, a phantom".

5   The Duhem–Quine thesis

The Duhem––Quine thesis refers to the works of the physicist Pierre Duhem (1906/1976) and the philosopher Willard van Orman Quine (1951). The article of Quine entitled "Two dogmas of empiricism" was one of the most influential philosophical articles of the 20th century and constituted a decisive element in the demise of the philosophical movement of logical positivism. The Duhem–Quine thesis argues that theories are webs of beliefs, and empirical evidence can only identify the edges of theories. Only few of the beliefs making up our theories are directly tied to empirical reality. The majority of beliefs remains deep within each web of beliefs and is therefore not directly accessible. Yet these beliefs are no less crucial than those beliefs that are empirically observable, as they can make up the entire fundament of the theory. This poses a problem for the falsification of theories, because, if a theory fails an empirical test, it becomes difficult or even impossible to track down where exactly in the web of beliefs that makes up the theory the error lies in. The empirical feedback we receive cannot be attributed to specific beliefs within the entire web, as any of the beliefs could have been false.

This difficulty to falsify a hypothesis can be expressed more formally. The Duhem–Quine thesis makes it much harder to apply the modus tollens. The modus tollens says that if a hypothesis H predicts an observation O, but the empirical test shows that there happens to be non-O, then researchers can infer backward that there must also be non-H. Because of their failure to find O, they can conclude that the initial hypothesis H was false, too. However, in a web of different hypotheses, every hypothesis H depends on one or several auxiliary hypotheses A. If H and A together predict O, but the empirical test shows that non-O, the conclusion that there needs to be non-H is invalid, because it could as well have been non-A, that is, the auxiliary hypothesis A could be false and not the hypothesis H.

The weak Duhem–Quine thesis corresponds more to the position of Duhem: to conclusively falsify a given hypothesis, one needs to show that there are no auxiliary hypotheses that can save it. This is of course difficult, as there exists always a potential ad-hoc fix that can save the main hypothesis. The strong Duhem–Quine thesis corresponds more to the position of Quine: to conclusively resist falsifying a given hypothesis, one needs to show that there is an auxiliary hypothesis that can save it. In Quine's (1951) terms: "Any statement can be held true come what may, if we make drastic enough adjustments elsewhere in the system". This means that auxiliary hypothesis can be actively misused as ad-hoc fixes to save the main hypothesis. Often, the limit to the introduction of such ad-hoc fixes is just the researchers' creativity.

The key insight of the Duhem–Quine thesis is for us that a hypothesis cannot be tested in isolation, because every hypothesis is always tied to several different auxiliary hypotheses. We can therefore often not falsify a given hypothesis, since it could have been one or more false auxiliary hypotheses that have led to the empirical evidence that seemingly falsified our hypothesis of interest.

The Duhem–Quine thesis is thus the inverse view of the garden of forking paths. Every auxiliary hypothesis à la Duhem–Quine corresponds to a decision about a researcher degree of freedom in the garden of forking paths. The network of auxiliary hypotheses researchers need in order to test a given hypothesis is thus equal to the way they walk along the garden of forking paths. This means that researchers do not just test an individual hypothesis but rather test their hypothesis in conjunction with the entire way through the garden of forking paths. The impossibility to test a given hypothesis in the sense of Duhem–Quine is only one side of the coin, whereas the numerous different empirical approaches in the literature, coupled with always different findings, is the other side of the same coin. As long as we observe large variation in feedback, we are also not able to falsify a theory.

The Duhem–Quine thesis also encompasses nondiversifiable background knowledge such as basic logic. In science in general, examples for auxiliary hypotheses are the theoretical abstractions of the theory, the laboratory setup, the instruments used for measuring, or the assumptions of statistical inference. Many of these auxiliary hypotheses can hardly be diversified away. Hence, the researcher can always only falsify a hypothesis in conjunction with all nondiversifiable auxiliary hypotheses.

The cause behind false feedback is the use of false auxiliary hypotheses. For example, in the history of the natural sciences it has happened often that an experiment falsified a well-known theory, only for the research community to find out later on that there were crucial problems in the experimental setup, where some of the auxiliary hypotheses were found to be false (Chalmers 2013). Once they corrected the false auxiliary hypotheses, the hypothesis of interest remained untouched.

To obtain true feedback, all auxiliary hypotheses need to be true. If one or several of them are false, there can be no more conclusive test of the hypothesis under investigation. Only a series of unambiguously true decisions along the way through the garden of forking paths delivers true feedback. However, in the previous chapter we argued that every such decision is true or false only in degree. Unfortunately, a series of mostly true and somewhat false decisions will lead to false feedback, and it remains impossible for us to predict how far from true feedback such an interrelated series of decisions will fall. Since the auxiliary hypotheses are partly false, the empirical feedback will be so, too.

Karl Popper (1972) answered to the difficulty the Duhem–Quine poses for falsification that in the natural sciences many crucial auxiliary hypotheses constitute unproblematic background knowledge we do not have to question again every time we proceed to an empirical test. For example, scientists may already know that a particular scientific instrument, for instance a microscope, works appropriately. If we know that our auxiliary hypotheses are true, we can also test the desired hypothesis in isolation and subject it to falsification. This may indeed work for some applications in the natural sciences, where the appropriate working of scientific instruments is often beyond doubt. In economics, in contrast, the different auxiliary hypotheses usually correspond to assumptions that are hidden within the context of the respective study, so we have no way of knowing whether they are indeed true or false. Thus, in economics, taking the way through the garden of forking paths as unproblematic background knowledge assumes the problem away and will not get us closer to true feedback.

Karl Popper's (1972) second answer was in a more practical spirit, namely that we should test our theories piecemeal, always one problem at a time, and that we should do the same for our critical auxiliary hypotheses, that we should test them in isolation from each other. Such a piecemeal approach allows mitigating the problem of conjoint hypotheses. However, Popper's answer is again more relevant for the natural sciences, where we can often double-check and, if necessary, manually fix relevant auxiliary hypotheses. Scientists can dissect scientific instruments to single out the influence of separate auxiliary hypothesis and check why the instruments as a whole do not function correctly. For example, to check whether a scientific instrument works, we can try it out on objects for which we know the relevant properties. If the instrument shows results that deviate from these properties, we have to correct it accordingly. Because scientific instruments are practical instruments, we receive true feedback about how to improve them. In economics, apart from the applied estimators, we can seldom double-check key auxiliary hypotheses, and even if we detect violations, we can often not fix them.

In empirical economics, the main tool we rely on to mitigate the problems surrounding the Duhem–Quine thesis are robustness checks. The target of robustness checks is to find out whether a particular auxiliary hypothesis has a strong influence on the obtained results, in the sense that the main results evaporate once the auxiliary hypothesis is relaxed. This is of special importance for those auxiliary hypotheses that seem arbitrary. If the results hold up under alternative forms of the auxiliary hypothesis, we can reject it as responsible for having generated the results, and it becomes less relevant whether this auxiliary hypothesis is in fact true or not. The more auxiliary hypotheses we can rule out as having a decisive influence, the more confidence we can have in our results, since it eliminates these as potential alternative explanations. Expressed differently, we can be confident that the tested auxiliary hypotheses were not producing a methodological artefact. However, within a given study, we can never test all our auxiliary hypotheses for their robustness, because some of them make up the fundament of the entire study. If researchers consider one such auxiliary hypotheses as critical, and want to check its robustness, they would need to pursue a very different study that relies on a set of different auxiliary hypotheses. We will take up again the issue of robustness checks in Chapter 13. For the moment, it is sufficient to hold in mind that robustness checks can show that a given finding holds up for alternative statistical specifications as well, meaning that different ways through the garden of forking paths produce similar findings, and the auxiliary hypotheses are therefore not decisive.

6   The detection of patterns

6.1 Specification searching

The chapter on the "garden of forking paths" discussed how the researcher degrees of freedom present in an empirical strategy can cause large variation in feedback. These researcher degrees of freedom thereby range from designing the study to collecting, cleaning, processing, and analyzing the data. In all of these steps, the leeway researchers have available in making alternative choices can lead to large variation in the obtained estimates. This chapter, in contrast, focuses more narrowly on only the last step in this chain: the data analysis. It discusses specification searching, the process of analyzing the data in many different ways until some set of researcher degrees of freedom leads to results that satisfy certain outcomes like statistical significance. Of course, the principle underlying specification searching can go well beyond just analyzing the data. It may reach back into all steps of collecting, cleaning, and processing the data and may even lead researchers to change their entire empirical strategy. Each time researchers are not satisfied with the obtained findings, they can implement changes in any step of the project. However, this deeper kind of searching for certain outcomes is cumbersome; changing influential researcher degrees of freedom located at the outset of the study implies substantial extra work, as it requires researchers to adapt everything following from them. This chapter thus focuses on the comparatively easier forms of specification searching, when the dataset is already prepared, and researchers leverage only those degrees of freedom available in the data analysis stage.

The frequentist approach to statistical inference demands that we test our hypotheses in one single shot. Researchers formulate an idea, use theory to derive a hypothesis, find adequate data, and test the hypothesis only once: either it passes the empirical test or it does not. If the data reject the hypothesis, researchers will need to start this same cycle from anew. The empirical feedback decides the fate of the hypothesis. The frequentist approach to statistical inference forbids respecifying the applied empirical model in order to achieve specific outcomes such as statistical significance.

The one-shot approach means that researchers need to have a clearly formulated plan about how to execute their empirical strategy in mind. It requires every researcher to derive the model specification for their empirical strategy before having seen the data, estimate it only once, and then keep all of the obtained empirical results, irrespective of how they turn out. The one-shot approach does not require that researchers blindly write down every single code line before even having seen the data. To the contrary, researchers will need to go first in detail through the entire dataset, to check whether it is cleaned appropriately or whether it still contain errors. For example, the researchers will need to check the descriptive information of all relevant variables and plot them in various different ways. Otherwise, important shortfalls of the data could go unnoticed, invalidating the entire empirical strategy right from the outset. However, researchers must not let this descriptive information influence their applied empirical model. The plan for the model specification pertaining to the empirical strategy needs to remain the same throughout and cannot be altered in light of the data anymore.

This ideal of writing down the exact empirical specification before even seeing the data is sometimes difficult to implement in practice, because the researchers will frequently not have access to exactly those data they need. In scientific practice, the researchers have an empirical strategy in mind, and when they obtain the dataset, they will often have to compromise and make the best out of what is available. This implies that in some instances researchers have no other option than to adapt the empirical strategy and proceed in a different direction, for example, if a certain variable is not part of the dataset or is measured in a different way than expected. Such modifications of the empirical strategy do not pose a problem for statistical inference, as long as researchers do not take into account the actual realizations of the data. It becomes a problem for statistical inference only if the researchers fit their empirical strategy to the observations at hand. That is, if they adapt their empirical specification such that it best fits the particular patterns observed in the dataset they have now access to.

However, every applied researcher knows that the one-shot approach, using only the ex-ante defined way through the garden of forking paths, does often not work out, since the quantities of interest will fall short of the required levels of statistical significance. In an ideal world, finding statistically insignificant results would not be a problem. P-values are only one among many factors of a study that jointly determine the usefulness of empirical evidence; other such equally important factors include "related prior evidence, plausibility of mechanism, study design and data quality, real-world costs and benefits, novelty of finding, and other factors that vary by research domain" (McShane et al. 2019a). Nevertheless, most academic journals will not publish findings that are not statistically significant. They see low p-values seldom as a sufficient, but almost always as a necessary condition for useful empirical evidence. Few editors and reviewers seem ready to embrace the uncertainty that comes along with higher p-values. Even though Wasserstein et al. (2019) conclude "'statistically significant' – don't say it and don't use it", academic journals will not abandon statistical significance that quickly. Most economists are aware that thresholds like $p < 0.05$ are arbitrary conventions and can vary in their usefulness. Yet they seek an "objective" decision criterion whether a given study is able to adequately distinguish real findings from random patterns. In a commendable act, the journals of the American Economic Association (AEA) have stopped the practice of highlighting statistically significant results with symbols such as asterisks. The absence of explicit thresholds like $p < 0.05$ would allow researchers better considering the context of the respective study. However, removing asterisks from result tables will not alter decades of thinking about statistical significance as a necessary condition for useful empirical evidence, and the research community will very likely continue to evaluate results by some implicit threshold of statistical significance. Unlike Socrates, most researchers seem not to attach much value to the knowledge that we don't know. The consequence of the ubiquitous requirement for statistical significance is that researchers anticipate it and therefore actively search for it.

The search for statistical significance has adverse consequences. Every researcher is aware of the problem of false positives. For example, a research field consisting of a hundred studies, which all meet a statistical significance threshold of 0.05, will in expectation contain five studies with spurious empirical findings. A false-positive rate of about five in a hundred does not sound very dramatic. However, searching for statistical significance massively increases this problem of false positives.

There is first the so-called "file drawer problem" (Sterling 1959, Rosenthal 1979, Denton 1985, De Long and Lang 1992, Card and Krueger 1995, Franco et al. 2014). Researchers who obtain statistically insignificant results in their tests of a given hypothesis know that they will not be able to publish these results and thus let them vanish in their "file drawers". Since other researchers do not know about those hidden, statistically insignificant results, they may be likely to repeat the very same hypothesis tests again, until finally some researcher hits upon a statistically significant result and is able to publish it, contributing nothing but a false positive to the literature.

The file drawer problem becomes worse if the collective effort invested into testing a given hypothesis is large. If 20 different researchers each run trials to test a hypothesis and 19 of them fail to obtain statistically significant results, while one succeeds, the latter researcher will be much more likely to publish the study of this particular hypothesis, and the research community will subsequently take it as evidence in line with the hypothesis. Numerous independent researchers testing the very same hypothesis make the file drawer problem worse; the more they are, the worse it becomes.

Rosenthal (1979) consequently describes the file drawer problem as the extreme scenario where all the tested hypotheses are false, and only those

5% turning up statistically significant become published, while the other 95% remaining statistically insignificant end up in the file drawer.

To quantify the extent of the file drawer problem is difficult, since file drawered studies are per definition invisible to the research community. The lack of knowledge about the universe of all pursued studies is exactly what constitutes the problem itself. Franco et al. (2014) provide an estimate from a special setup where they have access to a population of over 221 planned experiments in the social sciences. They find that over 60% of null results are not written up, and that only about 20% of null results become published eventually. Based on the results of Franco et al. (2014) we can only suppose that the file drawer problem is substantial; we are missing out on many null results.

However, we are here after a different, although closely related problem, namely the widespread practice of researchers to actively search for statistically significant results *within* a given study. Most applied researchers always try out large numbers of different model specifications on their data. If a particular specification turns out to be statistically insignificant, they simply drop it and move on to an alternative set of possible specifications. In the published article, they then only show their final specifications and omit all those alternative specifications that would have led to different findings.

The majority of researchers will therefore not just give up when their first hypothesis test produces an insignificant finding. When researchers have started out a project, they will also finish it somehow, since otherwise they will have wasted substantial resources.[1] As Ronald Coase put it: "If you torture the data enough, nature will always confess". Consequently, researchers closely scrutinize their data and reconfigure their specifications until they obtain a set of statistically significant results. Some researchers just give up if there is really no sign of any useable result in their data, after having tried out everything they can think of. The extent of the file drawer problem therefore depends heavily on the ability of researchers to make null results statistically significant. If researchers can always turn their results statistically significant, no study will end up in the file drawer. Before we can adequately address the file drawer problem, we thus have to focus on the practice of specification searching.

Specification searching is a broad term that includes not only the search for statistically significant results but also, for instance, improved model fit. The term p-hacking, in contrast, is narrower in scope and refers explicitly to the search for statistically significant results (Simonsohn et al. 2014). However, there are variations of p-hacking, too. Some forms of p-hacking have a higher likelihood to produce actual findings than others. Moreover, specification searching can also refer to other forms of searching for statistical significance, such as fishing and forking, which we will discuss below.

There is first a difference between fragile and robust p-hacking. Fragile p-hacking produces estimates that change substantially as soon as one alters a minor aspect in the statistical analysis. Fragile p-hacking is seldom justified. If the statistical significance disappears as soon as one changes some minor researcher degrees of freedom, the evidential value of the p-hacked estimate is very minor. Fragile p-hacking really only serves to force coefficients over the 0.05 threshold and make results publishable. In contrast, robust p-hacking can produce statistical models that hold up even to major changes in the statistical analysis. Robust p-hacking is justified if it is adequately distinguished as exploratory analysis (see Section 14.3). It can serve to uncover actual patterns in the data we can learn from. However, as the next chapters will show, robust p-hacking, as it is commonly practiced, is not unproblematic either.

Simonsohn (2020) further differentiates between slow and fast p-hacking. Slow p-hacking produces a p-value for the variable of interest that changes only little between successive trials. This is more often the case in research with large observational datasets, where, for instance, researchers exclude observations, perform transformations of a variable, or extent time periods (Simonsohn 2020). Since the data are large and the subsequent analyses similar, the p-value changes only slowly. Fast p-hacking, on the other hand, produces a p-value of the variable of interest that changes fast between successive trials. Simonsohn (2020) argues that this is more often the case in research with small experimental datasets. Consider, for instance, an experiment that has sampled many alternative outcomes. Substituting the outcomes between successive trials will change the p-value of the variable of interest drastically, because the underlying statistical tests are independent from each other.

Importantly, fast p-hacking does not necessarily deliver more fragile estimates than slow p-hacking. Researchers implicitly discount changes in empirical specifications as either major or minor. If an empirical model does not collapse because of some small adjustments, researcher do not perceive it as especially robust. In contrast, if the model does collapse, they will perceive it as very fragile. The reverse holds for large adjustments of the empirical model. If it collapses because of, for instance, a change in the outcome variable, this does not necessarily indicate high fragility, as the underlying theoretical implications may have changed, too. In contrast, if the empirical model does not collapse, researchers will perceive it as especially robust, as it holds up over different theoretical contexts.

Methods can also matter for p-hacking. Different research designs may provide more or less room for p-hacking, as they forbid certain choices of researcher degrees of freedom. Brodeur et al. (2020) investigate this possibility through collecting 21,000 hypotheses tests from articles published in 25 leading economic journals. They find that p-hacking greatly varies by method. As in Brodeur et al. (2016), they identify two-humped or camel-shaped distributions of test statistics for all research designs. However, instrumental variables approaches, and to a lesser degree difference-in-differences designs, show substantially more two-humped distributions (and thus p-hacking) than regression discontinuity designs and randomized controlled trials. The former seem to offer more researcher degrees of freedom than the latter. Especially RCTs seem less affected by forcing p-values just below the 0.05 threshold. However, Simonsohn (2020) points out that the approach of Brodeur et al. (2020) can only identify slow p-hacking. If researchers can resort to fast p-hacking, the distribution of p-values does not imply the characteristic two-humped or camel-shaped distribution identified by Brodeur et al. (2020). The distributions of test statistics generated by fast p-hacking are smooth and do not show crowding below the 0.05 threshold. Brodeur et al. (2020) may thus underestimate the actual extent of p-hacking. RCTs may be no better with respect to fast p-hacking than any other research design. In fact, Simonsohn (2020) argues that experiments are more prone to fast p-hacking. Nonetheless, the evidence of Brodeur et al. (2020) shows that RCTs at least fare better with respect to slow p-hacking.

An extreme form of specification searching is "fishing", which is a completely agnostic search for statistically significant results. Bettis (2012) tells us about the following incident:

> I asked an obviously talented second year PhD student at a top 25 business school the usual, uncreative conversation starter, "so what are you studying?" His reply of "I look for asterisks" momentarily confused me. He proceeded to tell me how as a research assistant under the direction of two senior faculty members he searched a couple of large databases for potentially interesting regression models within a general topical area with "asterisks" (10% or better significance levels) one some variables. When such models were found, he helped his mentor propose theories and hypotheses on the basis of which the "asterisks" could be explained.

Such an agnostic search for statistically significant results is almost by necessity bound to uncover numerous results that constitute nothing but statistical flukes.

There are also more subtle forms of specification searching. The garden of forking paths as introduced by Gelman and Loken (2013) contains a core aspect in this regard we have not discussed so far. They point out that researchers often base their decisions about which researcher degrees of freedom to choose on the particular dataset they are looking at. Yet different datasets contain different patterns of statistical noise. Since researchers are likely to make at least some of their decisions based on the dataset they observe, the different noise patterns present in the different datasets can lead to substantial differences in the decisions made. For instance, a researcher's course of action could be influenced by the realized distributions of the variables in his dataset. An example here is that the researcher looks at the distribution of a variable in his dataset and then decides based on this information how to categorize it into dummy variables. Although the researcher may have chosen reasonably given his or her particular dataset, he or she may have chosen differently based on other datasets. Data analytic decisions can be endogenous to the respective dataset. Thus, even if researchers do not explicitly p-hack, they may nevertheless implicitly make data analytic decisions based on the statistical noise present in only their dataset. To cancel out the influence of such noise patterns on the decisions of researchers, one would need to average out over all the potential realizations of the dataset. Otherwise, researchers may be surfing on the statistical noise present only in their respective dataset.

Importantly, the different forms of specification searching, namely p-hacking, fishing, and forking are all interwoven. They are alternative manifestations of the very same problem, and all of them cause an increase in the false-positive rate. Together they amplify and complement each other in the search for statistical significance. For instance, researchers might first fall prey to forking in their pursuit to identify promising features of the data. They then resort to fishing, in order to isolate statistically significant results from the abundant material the data provide. Finally, they use p-hacking to seal the deal of sufficiently high statistical significance for the most promising outcomes.

Nevertheless, we can try to rank the different forms of specification searching according to how detrimental they are for the literature and how bad they are in terms of the intentions of the researchers (see Table 6.1). They do differ in the adverse consequences they have for the literature and also in whether researchers are aware of these adverse consequences. Many researchers act in good faith, especially when they pursue robust p-hacking, because they do not fully understand that their practices are of a problematic nature. They p-hack because they simply do not know any better.

Fishing is probably the most problematic form of specification searching. An agnostic search for statistical significance contributes a broad range of "findings" to the literature that are of very unclear value. It distorts the theoretical stand of the literature with sometimes more plausible, other times less plausible "effects". Fragile p-hacking, in contrast, typically starts out from a more solid theoretical background. It serves to enforce statistically significant results for a certain hypothesis. If only special combinations of researcher degrees of freedom show statistical significance, the data do not provide enough power to reject the null hypothesis though. The result is the contribution of a "finding" to the literature that is most likely either

Table 6.1 Different forms of specification searching

Adverse consequences	Bad intentions
Fishing	Fragile p-hacking
Fragile p-hacking	Fishing
Forking	Robust p-hacking
Robust p-hacking	Forking

nonexistent or much weaker. In contrast to fishing, the range of implausible findings fragile p-hacking contributes to the literature is narrower, as it can profit from a more solid starting point. The adverse consequences of forking depend on the signal-to-noise ratio in the dataset. In datasets with a high signal-to-noise ratio, exploration of the dataset with, for instance, alternative graphical plots is even likely to guide the researcher in the right direction. In noisy datasets, however, forking can lead to strongly misleading results, as the researcher will fit statistical noise patterns that are very unlikely to generalize. Robust p-hacking is in many instances least problematic and comes most closely to a solid exploratory analysis. It serves to unearth clear patterns in the data that can uphold the scrutiny of other researchers. Robust p-hacking is least problematic if the findings integrate well into the existing literature. However, robust p-hacking can hit on spurious results in the data, too, as the repeated testing underlying it invalidates the displayed p-values (see Section 6.3).

In terms of the bad intentions of researchers, fragile p-hacking is worst. Researchers who pursue fragile p-hacking realize that their data are not sufficient to provide evidence for their preferred hypothesis and nevertheless force the data to show otherwise. Almost all economists would agree that a p-hacked, fragile result is not of much value. Those researchers that nonetheless pursue fragile p-hacking thus clearly act with bad intentions. The problem with fishing is that many researchers do not fully understand that it could be problematic, as they take the obtained statistical significance levels at face value. These researchers tend to think that they have indeed found novel results that are valuable contributions to the literature. With fishing, the problem is more a lack of awareness. Most economists consider robust p-hacking, even if combined with fishing, as even less problematic, as this is the bread and butter of most applied researchers, who intensely mine their data in a thorough way such that they find seemingly strong patterns in the data. They are not aware that repeated testing invalidates p-values. One can thus also hardly attribute bad intentions to them, as it is the standard practice in most applied research. Forking is even more subtle in this regard. Researchers can even be aware that testing multiple specifications invalidates p-values and just because of this explicitly plot the data in various ways, in order to find promising starting points. Researchers are even encouraged to do so in order to avoid running estimations as black boxes. Forking is thus almost inevitable. The common credo is to learn about the data first. Forking is thus commonly done with the least bad intentions.

In the following chapters, we will concentrate mostly on robust p-hacking. If we talk about fragile p-hacking, it is explicitly mentioned as such. However, we implicitly assume that robust p-hacking is often accompanied by forking and sometimes also by fishing. As indicated, the three often work in tandem with each other, whereby robust p-hacking has the lead, as it serves to hammer out the final model specification that aligns well with the demands of either the research design or the applied theory.

6.2 P-hacking in practice

The skilled p-hacker uses all of the researcher degrees of freedom she has available to explore her dataset in every detail. Naturally, she will first set on a journey to discover the data and inspect all kinds of descriptive statistics, tables, graphs, tests, and simple specifications. This way she gathers information about potential starting points for her search for an adequate specification. Importantly, the first attempt to fit the statistical model almost never works. The p-hacker merely uses this first attempt for her intense ensuing search. At every potentially consequential forking path, the p-hacker goes through all of the available researcher degrees of freedom that seem theoretically defensible, tests them out, and then chooses the one degree of freedom that produces the most significant results. If at a given forking path all available researcher degrees of freedom fail to produce satisfactory results, she moves back one or more forking paths and tries out alternative, equally defensible ways that avoid this specific set of researcher degrees of freedom. In case these alternative ways exert a large influence on all other chosen researcher degrees of freedom, the p-hacker may have to adapt the entire way she has chosen so far through the garden of forking paths. The p-hacker pursues this approach until she gets a significant final specification that holds up to all kinds of robustness checks. That is, she will choose a statistical model that lays within a set of relatively similar models, all of them showing sufficiently statistically significant results. If she fails in discovering such a model, she will start from scratch again and try out different attempts to fit the statistical model. The skilled p-hacker will only stop her endeavor once she has obtained a set of robust specifications that meet her outcome criteria well.

In a smaller project, the p-hacker can try to get an overview over all possible ways through the garden of forking paths by walking each of them to the end. Ideally, the estimates will agree more or less with each other. In practice, they most often do not. In either case the p-hacker will select those ways through the garden of forking paths that show up most significant. Notably, when a project is part of one larger project, p-hacking can prove problematic, because other parts of the same project may interact with the chosen ways through the garden of forking paths. The different small projects may require ways to achieve statistical significance that differ from or even contradict each other.

Looking for potential errors is of course key during every data analysis. Data may be wrongly coded or an estimation may not work properly. Correcting such errors is not only valid but absolutely necessary. When working with the data, good empirical researchers summarize the data after every single step, to check whether they may have committed some error, or whether the data deliver indeed what they have expected. However, the path between correcting errors and p-hacking is often a narrow one; researchers always detect instances in their data they did not anticipate. And they always find good reasons for why specific instances working against their preferred results should be counted as errors, while in fact they are merely alternative ways to formulate the statistical model.

Similarly, when researchers p-hack to search for empirical evidence supporting their ex-ante formulated theoretical arguments, they naturally judge their obtained findings by how closely they correspond to the outcomes they have expected. Many researchers therefore meander through the degrees of freedom they have available until they consider the obtained findings more credible. They misuse the leeway in the garden of forking paths to cherry-pick evidence, often unconsciously, until they hit on some specifications that are in line with their theoretical arguments, neglecting or explaining away specifications that point into alternative directions. As long as the findings look implausible, they continue to search for potential misspecifications of the applied statistical model, but once the findings look credible, that is, the findings approach the researchers' ex-ante perspectives, then they believe to have solid empirical evidence in their hands.

The intuition of experienced economists about the potential magnitude of an economic effect can certainly be valuable in preventing false feedback. However, valid economic intuition can actually become counterproductive in the hands of a p-hacker. If a researcher p-hacks down too large effects or p-hacks up too small effects by arbitrarily exploiting her available researcher degrees of freedom, she will obtain nothing but empty conformations that will not provide any insights into why she did not discover the true effect. Given one's intuition about economics is indeed pretty accurate, an unrealistically large or small estimate cries out for a sizable misspecification of the applied model. Simply p-hacking it away adds nothing to scientific understanding. The observation of an unrealistically large or small estimate requires to think through again very carefully all the methodological choices and maybe even to start the entire project from anew (which, of course, only few do). The misuse of the garden of forking paths to make effects more credible does not correspond to any useful empirical test. Such a p-hacked specification will only mislead others in the search for the best approach.

In fact, a researcher's intuition may in many instances point into the right direction, but it is unlikely to provide an accurate prediction of the magnitude of the estimated effect. An imprecise intuition about an economic effect is a double-edged sword. If the researcher sets out to adapt the statistical model to match her intuition, correct intuition could at least in principle rightfully initiate a legitimate search for misspecification of the statistical model. Incorrect intuition, on the other hand, opens the door to an only seemingly justified search for misspecifications that will merely increase false feedback. Thus, making results more credible is a narrow path between a legitimate search for model misspecification and an illusory justification to implement arbitrary changes to the statistical model. In general, the more imprecise a researcher's intuition about a given effect, the higher the expected variation in false feedback will be, as it increases the meandering to match the intuition.

A simple test to detect whether you may be unknowingly p-hacking is to ask yourself whether you would also have performed these same modifications in researcher degrees of freedom had the p-values increased. For instance, given an outcome is statistically insignificant, you may search for possible errors or misspecifications in your analysis and find critical researcher degrees of freedom that move the results into the "right" direction. You would then need to ask yourself whether you would also have performed these same changes in researcher degrees of freedom if the results had moved in the opposite direction. The idea is not to fall prey to hindsight bias; after observing that it "works", any modification seems reasonable. The only way out is to imagine a counterfactual situation where results would have become less statistically significant. Of course, this test is useful only to make self-deception elicit, if a researcher is intentionally p-hacking, it becomes superfluous.

In any case, p-hackers omit a lot of relevant evidence in their studies, as they present only their most stable and most robust results. For example, they show only the nicest difference-in-differences setting, the nicest experimental setup, the nicest instrumental variable setting, or the nicest regression discontinuity design they have uncovered during their intense searches. All other trials on the data are silently omitted from the study. The question is now of course how large the evidential value of such robustly p-hacked results in fact is. The next chapter will show that this value can be very low.

6.3 Multiple comparisons

Even robustly p-hacked, statistically significant results are in many cases merely a consequence of an intricate interplay of statistical noise. Inference in null hypothesis testing is valid only if it is carried out once, in one single shot. Trial and error relying on many alternative ways to analyze the data and then picking the most significant ways leads to severely distorted statistical inference. For instance, using the 5% significance threshold, 100 tests of independent, always true null hypotheses will, in expectation, produce five statistically significant results. If a researcher tries out a large number of ways how to analyze the data, the actual rate of spurious results will be much higher than these 5%. In the above example, the probability of obtaining at least one false positive reaches an extreme value of 99.4%.

P-hacking is thus much more problematic than the file drawer. The file drawer describes a situation where the same hypothesis is tested on many datasets, while p-hacking describes a situation where many hypotheses are tested on the same dataset. Each renewed trial runs in both cases a risk of discovering a false positive. However, in the case of the file drawer, researchers start out an entire project to test their newest trial, which is very time consuming. In contrast, in the case of p-hacking, researchers can test their new trials within seconds. The problem lies in this huge difference in time spans: p-hacking produces false positives at a rate orders of magnitudes faster than the file drawer. The most prolific p-hackers squeeze the one dataset they hold in their hands until it finally delivers significant results; p-hacking is thus almost guaranteed to deliver false positives. In a scenario of only true null hypotheses and extreme p-hacking, using a 5% significance threshold, the file drawer produces an expected five false positives in the same time p-hacking can produce a full 100 false positives.

P-hacking pursues by repeatedly drawing estimates from a dataset, each time with a new opportunity to "discover" a statistically significant result. The chances to obtain significant estimates are maximal if the trials are independent, since then they can leverage statistical noise the most.

The instance when several statistical tests are considered simultaneously is called "multiple comparisons problem". There exist different methods to adjust p-value thresholds for multiple comparisons. The simplest but also most conservative methods are Bonferroni and Šidàk corrections (see, e.g., Abdi 2007). Given independent, always true null hypotheses, the Šidàk correction provides the family-wise error rate "f", which is the probability of at least one error given all the pursued trials, by the following formula $f=1-(1-a)^c$, where "a" is the initial statistical significance threshold, and "c" is the number of independent trials (see Table 6.2). The Šidàk correction relies on the fact that the joint probability of independent trials run to achieve statistical significance is the product of their probabilities. The Bonferroni correction relies on a similar, even simpler formula of $f=a/c$. One can see from these formulas that the actual statistical significance level "f" decreases sharply in the number of independent trials "c".

Lovell (1983) provides a rule of thumb for the case of data mining (what is today called p-hacking) with several explanatory variables. The formula of Lovell is related to the Šidàk correction. A search for combinations of "k" variables out of a total number of "c" variables renders the individual

Table 6.2 Illustration of the family-wise error rate according to the Šidàk correction

Targeted significance threshold: 0.10					
Number of trials	1	5	10	20	100
Family-wise error rate "f" (i.e., the actual probability of at least one error)	0.100	0.410	0.651	0.878	1.000
Targeted significance threshold: 0.05					
Number of trials	1	5	10	20	100
Family-wise error rate "f" (i.e., the actual probability of at least one error)	0.050	0.226	0.401	0.642	0.994
Targeted significance threshold: 0.01					
Number of trials	1	5	10	20	100
Family-wise error rate "f" (i.e., the actual probability of at least one error)	0.010	0.049	0.096	0.182	0.634

variables statistically significant at a level of only $f=1-(1-a)^{c/k}$. The wider the search space "c" and the lower the number of chosen variables "k", the more likely the search will discover a false positive.

Benjamini and Hochberg (1995) offer an alternative method for adjustments for multiple comparisons. Their approach is especially valuable in the presence of a large number of simultaneous hypotheses tests, as they offer more power than Bonferroni or Šidàk corrections. If researchers want to make as many discoveries as possible, controlling for the probability of any error is unnecessarily stringent. If a small proportion of errors is not too costly, they will not affect the conclusions about the effectiveness of a treatment much. More specifically, Benjamini and Hochberg (1995) argue for controlling the false discovery rate (FDR), which they define as the expected number of false positives divided by the number of rejections of the null.[2] However, in economics, simultaneous testing of many hypotheses is much less common than sequential testing. P-hacking implies testing one model specification after another until one obtains a set of final specifications that cross the statistical significance threshold with a comfortable bolster. The path taken toward these estimations, which comprises all less significant estimates, is less relevant, as researchers will anyway omit them from their analyses. The gain of the Benjamini and Hochberg (1995) method to main-tain more marginally significant estimate is of less interest, as we anyway only focus on the core specifications, that is, the most significant ones. We can thus pursue more stringent procedures such as Bonferroni and Šidàk corrections.

In fact, 100 trials are in most instances a very low boundary. If programs like R or Stata contained a counter of the number of times a researcher clicked the "execute" button during a research project, this number would usually be in the several thousands. The search for the "right" specifica-tion of a statistical model can take dozens of hours. However, most of the trials in a specification search will be correlated and cluster around those researcher degrees of freedom exerting a large impact. If trials are correlated, Bonferroni and Šidàk corrections are too conservative. Since a series of dependent trials produces less variation in the test statistics than a series of independent trials, they correspond to fewer effective trials. One solution would be to substitute "c" in the Šidàk correction, $f=1-(1-a)^c$, with an estimate of the effective number of trials. Hence, the number of times the researcher clicks "execute" in the statistical program would be too high to apply it to these strict corrections.

For instance, in a setting of only true null hypotheses, the lower the correl-ation between two alternative dependent variables is, the higher the chances to obtain a statistically significant result that is a false positive. If the two dependent variables are not correlated, they offer more statistical noise to exploit. If, on the other hand, they are correlated, they measure something similar and therefore offer fewer new opportunities to exploit noise and to obtain statistical significance.

Most multiple comparisons corrections are designed for a use with multiple outcome variables, multiple explanatory variables, or multiple interaction effects. List et al. (2019) provide a test that can simultaneously account for combinations of all three. Unlike Bonferroni and Šidàk corrections, their test can account for the dependence structure between the variables. Their procedure is thus much more efficient, as it considers only the effective number of trials. However, multiple comparisons procedures for alternative combinations of variables can address the problem of p-hacking only partially, since the garden of forking paths, including all silent steps, goes far beyond the choice of variables.

In their famous article, Simmons et al. (2011) run simulations to assess the impact of four common researcher degrees of freedom on obtaining at least one false positive: a) choosing among dependent variables, b) choosing sample size, c) using covariates, and d) reporting subsets of experimental conditions. They asses the influence of each of these in isolation and, importantly, in combination. Because researcher degrees of freedom interact, their combination increases the probability of detecting at least one false positive massively. In their simulation, independent variation of the four researcher degrees of freedom increases the chance of obtaining at least one result significant at the 0.05 threshold to about 10%. In contrast, when all four researcher degrees of freedom are varied together, the chance to obtain at least one significant result increases to over 60%. To obtain adequate multiple comparisons corrections for such researcher degrees of freedom as sample size or covariates is difficult. This is also the reason Simmons et al. (2011) chose simulations to illustrate the problem.

Consequently, the multiple comparisons problem discussed in this section is more of an illustration of the underlying problem of repeated trials than an adequate solution for it. Actual empirical analysis is often messy and does not allow for a clean division into separate (effective) trials. Moreover, researchers make many decisions endogenous to their respective dataset, based on the actual realizations of their data, such that multiple comparisons corrections come in too late; the numerous specification decisions have already been made implicitly and before such a formal correction could even have taken place. Correction for multiple comparisons makes probably most sense in the context of pre-analysis plans, which are discussed in Section 14.3. When researchers pre-specify their ways through the garden of forking paths ex-ante, they can incorporate multiple comparison corrections for, for example, the separate outcome variables they plan to analyze, such as in List et al. (2019).

The central problem is that most applied researchers do not quite realize that their p-hacked results are subject to invalid p-values. They deem their high t-statistics as nearly irrefutable evidence in favor of their hypotheses. These researchers are not aware that a valid statistical significance test would require an adjustment for all of the pursued, effective trials, which would produce a much lower p-value of only $a=1-(1-f)^{1/c}$. Of course, as indicated, most of their pursued trials will be heavily correlated; when, for instance, a researcher fits some core model and tries to improve it to obtain a robust final specification. However, even in a modest instance of only 10 independent trials until the final specification, it already requires an adjustment of the 0.05 significance threshold to a 0.005 threshold. A majority of the existing, published studies would not survive this more stringent threshold.

The problem of p-hacking becomes worse once one accounts for the asymmetry in the selection of p-values. Taleb (2016) describes p-hacking as an option on statistical significance that benefits from the underlying variance of the distribution of p-values. Since the p-hacker can choose the most favorable p-value out of all of the produced p-values, a higher variance in p-values serves to his advantage. The p-hacker cannot lose through high p-values and only win through low p-values. Because the distribution of p-values of non-zero effects is right skewed, with the mass of the observations concentrated at the left of the distribution, Taleb (2016) argues that most p-values observed in published studies are heavily overestimated. In his example, for a true p-value of 0.12, 60% of realized p-values will lie below the 0.05 significance threshold. In every trial, the p-hacker therefore faces a 60% probability of observing a statistical significant result at the 0.05 threshold, even if the true p-value is only 0.12. Because the p-hacker can simply discard all high p-values from the tail of the distribution, they have no opportunity to compensate for the right skewed distribution and to raise the p-value again toward its true value. The p-values observed in a p-hacked study can thus not be taken at face value even in instances of only minimal selection, since the true p-value will generally be much higher.

6.4 Underdetermination

In case a researcher found a suitable identification strategy, extensive p-hacking is likely to increase false feedback. Each type of identification strategy constrains the empirical model to follow a certain structure and thus allows less room for valid searches through the garden of forking paths. If an identification strategy does not deliver the desired results, p-hacking is then often merely an ex-post fix to make the identification strategy work out again. If a researcher thought long and hard about a subject and after some time indeed comes up with an ingenious way to identify causality, he or she also wants it to produce meaningful empirical results. If the results turned out to be insignificant, the sunk costs would be too large to just drop the entire identification strategy. Researchers then proceed to bending their applied data analysis until they can unearth at least some useful findings from the dataset.

However, more experienced researchers are sometimes able to detect results pushed through by p-hacking, especially if the applied statistical model violates logical considerations. Every formulated statistical model makes a set of precise statements. P-hackers at times choose a series of modeling decisions that, given the context of the empirical strategy, is highly inadequate. In such cases, p-hackers are often not actually estimating what they claim to be estimating, for example, when they oversee that one of the included explanatory variables changes the interpretation of the variable of interest in some fundamental way. Nonetheless, other researchers can evaluate the choices made in the garden of forking paths only up to a certain extent. If researchers test a theoretically more isolated hypothesis, the majority of all possible forking paths will remain unverifiable for others.

Most studies are accompanied by a theoretical background. Formulating a theory assures that the framework for the empirical study is well thought through; it states explicitly the theoretical assumptions and the relevant mechanisms behind the applied empirical strategy, such that others become aware what exactly we are talking about. Every empirical strategy needs a background against which it can be evaluated. Writing down a coherent theory makes the study much more transparent.

If a study is integrated within a well-formulated theory, other researchers will be better able to determine whether the applied econometric model is adequate or not, since they can often derive the right specification choices directly from the theory. If, in contrast, there exists substantial indeterminacy in the link between theory and empirics, that is, the theoretical setting of the study is relatively vague, results pushed through by p-hacking will be harder to detect. The room researchers have in choosing their econometric model thus depends on how many of the choices in the garden of forking paths the theory allows or forbids. If the theory is very precise, other researchers can better verify the appropriate econometric model. If the theory allows a lot of room for discretionary choice, on the other hand, it becomes difficult for them to pin down the appropriate model, such that researchers can just pick their preferred specifications.

A precise theory can also determine how the identification strategy should be implemented. In contrast, if there is no theory that specifies, for instance, how the treatment variable should look in the respective context, researchers can simply choose its most significant operationalization.

A precisely formulated theory thus specifies many choices in the garden of forking paths; for example, which explanatory variables have to be included and how exactly they should relate to each other. A very precise theory can determine many researcher degrees of freedom by requiring researchers to make a decision in favor of X and against Y. In contrast, a broadly formulated theory allows deliberate choice of a great many more researcher degrees of freedom than would already have been present with a very precise theory. A broad theory is in line with way too many different econometric models. All kinds of specifications of the applied model will count as evidence for or against such a vague theory. Empirical evidence is thus underdetermined through a broadly formulated theory.

In philosophy of science, underdetermination refers to the aspect of the Duhem–Quine thesis that theory is underdetermined through empirical evidence. It describes the problem that there exist many different theories able to fit a given empirical pattern. If researchers detect an interesting pattern in their data and go back to search the theoretical literature, they will likely find many alternative theoretical explanations for it. The same empirical evidence might be in line with different theories.

The observation that broadly formulated theories allow room for different empirical specifications implies that empirical evidence can be underdetermined through theory, too, in the sense that more than one way through the garden of forking paths seems adequate; there may even exist thousands of such seemingly adequate paths. These alternative ways will of course not all be equally true but rather all be equally unverifiable. However, even if they were all equally true, all the different findings will never point into the same direction, creating a wide array of potential matches between theory and empirical evidence. For example, if 200 ways through the garden of forking paths seem adequate, but only 100 of those 200 paths are statistically significant, researchers will be inclined to choose some set of the 100 statistically significant paths. Thus, even if all these 200 ways through the garden of forking paths were equally true, such a proceeding would grossly misrepresent the available empirical evidence, because there are as many statistically insignificant results as statically significant results. The researchers omit crucial information about the uncertainty of their estimates. Things get worse when they leave out series of forking paths that point into the opposite direction of the presented results. Unfortunately, it happens quite often that at least some specifications will show such contradictory findings. Hence, underdetermined empirical evidence is problematic because researchers have a lot of room to push through their preferred, statistically most significant specifications. The underdetermination through a broadly formulated theory makes it impossible to pin down an appropriate econometric model, and other researchers cannot identify such arbitrary series of choices.

The room for maneuver in the garden of forking paths therefore depends crucially on how the econometric model and the formulated theory relate to each other. Studies that present only a few references to theory and then move directly to the empirical part leave the largest room. Theoretical arguments in the form of text or stylized models capturing the intuition constrain the specification of the applied modelalready somewhat. The room for maneuver is tightest if the specification of the econometric model is derived from a theoretical model, where the structures of the two equations directly map onto each other.

To what extent are studies in economics accompanied by a theoretical background? Card et al. (2011) investigate the role of theory in experiments in the top five economic journals over the years 1975–2010. The number of both field and laboratory experiments in these five journals has strongly risen over this period. Card et al. (2011) examine whether the published experiments also rely on a theoretical model. 68% of field experiments lack any explicit model, while for laboratory experiments this rate is 46%. Card et al. (2011) argue that formulating a model makes assumptions explicit, clarifies mechanisms, and may even lead to further insights. Such guidance extends to the formulation of the econometric model. Nonetheless, the majority of experiments lacks such a theoretical background.

Popper (1959) calls the class of empirical observations allowed by a theory its "range". In line with our argumentation, he defines the range as the "amount of free play or the degree of freedom" the theory allows. The range of a theory stands in reverse relationship to its falsifiability. If a theory has a small range, it contains a large number of potential falsifiers, and there will be many opportunities for it to be refuted, as it forbids a large number of empirical observations. The theory risks more, it sticks its neck further out. In contrast, if a theory has a large range and allows a large number of empirical observations, it is much harder to falsify. Popper thus argues that precisely formulated theories are to be preferred over broadly formulated theories, because they assert more about the empirical world and can escape falsification less well. This maxim implies that a test of an econometric model derived from a theory expressed in mathematical form is more severe than a test of an econometric model derived from a more broadly formulated theory. In the latter case, there is few commitment and results from all kinds of model specifications are in line with the theory.

6.5 Reverse engineering

The degree of indeterminacy in the link between theory and empirics always reaches a limit. Even a very broadly formulated theory does never provide endless room for valid searches through the garden of forking paths. If the econometric model deviates too strongly from the theory, it will start to look implausible to other researchers. Moreover, if most of the omitted econometric models are statistically insignificant, the path chosen through the garden of forking paths will be fragile. In contrast, if researchers have the possibility to not only adapt their econometric model, but their theory, too, then p-hacking will become a powerful tool to discover seemingly strong links between theory and empirical evidence.

Similarly, if an effect is nonexistent or weak, or even points in the opposite direction, it is very difficult to make it robust. Forcing only one estimate to cross the $p < 0.05$ threshold is almost always possible. However, this type of p-hacking produces very fragile estimates that evaporate after only minimal changes in the specification. To get an entire set of statistically significant estimates, researchers need to look for an alternative story.

Reverse engineering theory through p-hacking is a step-by-step process, where the theoretical conjectures coevolve with the findings. The p-hackers continuously adapt their theoretical conjectures to the statistical results they obtain. The newly gained theoretical conjectures then serve as a basis for the trial of further specifications, and so forth. Only after extensive p-hacking, when the theoretical conjectures form a coherent whole, the researchers will start to write down the theoretical arguments they have distilled from the data.

Notably, no researcher approaches the data theory-blind. Researchers need to be guided by at least some theoretical conjectures before they can pursue successful p-hacking. Theory-blind p-hacking hardly works, as there is too much information available in every dataset. Researchers need at least some relevant knowledge where they have to look in the data to obtain theoretically meaningful patterns. Skilled p-hackers know exactly how to navigate the entire garden of forking paths; they are able to uncover robust patterns in their data providing evidence in line with coherent theories.

If the p-hacker finally discovers a strong association between both theory and empirics, robustness checks will not be very helpful anymore, even though the association may thrive on nothing but statistical noise. Robustness checks can detect fragile p-hacking but not when a researcher has hit on a strong spurious pattern in the data. Simonsohn (2016) presents an example of evidence for an "effect" that is necessarily a false positive, yet proves robust to alternative specifications. He looks for "interesting" correlations in the 2010 wave of the General Social Survey (GSS), a sample with more than 650 observations. Simonsohn (2016) shows that people who received an odd numbered identifier in the dataset are more likely to read the horoscope. The estimates have p-values well below 0.01. However, since the identifier was randomly assigned by the researchers after the collection of the data, people could not possibly have reacted to this "treatment". Nevertheless, the detected "effect" hardly changes across alternative specifications, despite the marked increases in R-squared.

Westling (2011) uncovers an "intriguing statistical artefact" in an obviously ironical article, which nevertheless amassed over 175,000 downloads in just a few weeks. He "finds" that length of the male organ can explain 20% of the between-country variation in GDP growth rates between 1960 and 1985. The male organ length is highly statistically significant and robust to alternative specifications. It is even more strongly associated with GDP growth than the country's political regime type. Westling (2011) argues that "The existence and channel of causality remains obscure at this point but the correlations are robust". This article nicely demonstrates how successful exercises of fitting statistical noise can be. If male organ length had been any other, more economically relevant variable, researchers would probably have taken it seriously and added it to the list of potential growth determinants. Westling (2011) himself argues that male organ length may proxy for some latent country characteristics. However, most likely is that it does not proxy for anything but statistical noise. All this article can show is that a great many other articles in empirical economics must be equally false, too.

Reverse engineering may extend to the entire research design as well. In general, research designs need to be credible ex-ante, such that other researchers buy into the identified effects. However, some rhetorically skilled researchers manage to present their research designs in such good light that even vaguely identified effects become credible. They simply p-hack a robust research design and then argue forcefully why it should be the right one. Of course, this problem is limited in that only few researchers indeed manage to sell such shaky research designs to top journals.

In the case of experiments, researchers can also p-hack by using, for example, a series of pretests and then choosing the entire experimental setup in line with the preliminary results they have obtained. When researchers have run several pretests, they can easily design the final experiment in such a way that they obtain what they want. This implies p-hacking not just in the analysis of the data, but already in the data generating process itself.

In most datasets, the variables present already provide numerous opportunities for p-hacking and then reverse engineering theory. While, for example, experimental setups can usually profit from statistical models with a relatively simple structure, they do not themselves restrict the available researcher degrees of freedom in the choices of the relevant variables. In experimental studies researchers usually collect many different variables, which can, in principle, all be tested out in the subsequent empirical analysis. This allows researchers choosing from various possible combinations of outcome variables, moderating variables, transformations of variables, control variables to achieve balance, subgroups with particular characteristics, or even different treatments conditions. At least some out of these many possible variable combinations will certainly turn out statistically significant.

Wicherts et al. (2016) put together a checklist to avoid p-hacking for experiments with an internally valid design, in the sense that "the experiment does not involve any confounds or artifacts and uses appropriate measures". They list a total of 34 researcher degrees of freedom in planning, running, analyzing, and reporting the study. A simple structure of the statistical model, like it is the case for experiments, is thus not itself sufficient to protect a study from extensive p-hacking.

The question is of course whether there is any evidence for the existence of arbitrary p-hacking, where alternative dependent and independent variables are freely recombined until a statistically significant result comes up. Such an agnostic search for statistical significance is what we have termed "fishing". The statistical material in Brodeur et al. (2016) may also allow us to give an answer to this question. Brodeur et al. (2016) generate four distributions of test statistics from four datasets: the WDI, QCG, PSID, and VHLSS. They randomly draw variables within each dataset, run 2 million regressions between these variables, and always collect the z-statistic behind the first explanatory variable. When compared to these four artificially generated distributions, the actual distribution of test statistics from the AER, QJE, and JPE lacks numerous low (i.e., statistically insignificant) test statistics and exhibits the characteristic bump of test statistics just below the 0.05 threshold, which Brodeur et al. identify as p-hacking. However, overall (i.e., without the bump), the artificial distribution of test statistics from the four datasets comes quite close to the actual distribution of test statistics from the published articles. The test statistics from the published articles would thus in principle be consistent with even an extreme (and arguably unrealistic) pattern of arbitrary p-hacking or fishing. The large majority of test statistics generated through the randomly complied regressions from the four datasets in Brodeur et al. (2016) would certainly correspond to false feedback, as they are the coefficients of highly endogenous relationships. Nevertheless, they map the actual distribution of test statistics from the published articles quite well.

Identifying theoretical arguments ex-post requires high flexibility in posing research questions. It resembles the image of a gunman who shoots randomly at a wall and then draws targets around the spots where he hit the wall, claiming that he intended to hit those spots right from the outset. Kerr (1998) calls the instance when researchers use results to decide what hypothesis to advance in the introduction Hypothesizing After the Results are Known (HARKing). He defines HARKing as "presenting a post hoc hypothesis (i.e., one based on or informed by one's results) in one's research report as if it were, in fact, an a priori hypotheses". HARKing masks theoretical arguments formulated ex-post and presents them as having been formulated ex-ante, thereby inverting the entire research process.

Kerr (1998) argues that, in principle, Bayesian reasoning would not prohibit using data for the generation of post hoc hypotheses. One could still use the evidence from all the studies that had already been available before the HARKing and counterfactually estimate the prior probability of the post hoc hypothesis being true. Using Bayes' theorem, this prior probability would then serve to estimate the posterior probability of the post hoc hypothesis. That is, how much belief we can have in the HARKed hypothesis given the new evidence. This line of thought would make HARKing no worse than a confirmatory analysis. However, Kerr (1998) doubts that a researcher who HARKs will evaluate the literature in the same way as when he takes a thorough ex-ante perspective, because the knowledge of the new results will likely bias the perception of the relevant literature. In more extreme words, if a researcher indeed finds an interesting pattern in the data, he will be convinced to have made a major discovery and will not let himself down by all of the complications posed by the previous literature.

The advantage of reverse engineering, when combined with robust p-hacking, is a flexible exploratory search to discover new findings. It is comparable to a walk into a little known territory. Researchers may have an existing map of the territory available, but once they walk into the territory, they find that it looks very different from their map. Where the researchers expected a lake, they actually find a forest; where they expected a mountain, they find a valley, and so forth. Unlike the targets drawn ex-post by the gunman, a report about beforehand unknown territory can unearth new knowledge, sometimes even more so than if everything fell into line with expectations.

In contrast, the advantage of the ex-ante approach is a deep thinking about a given problem of interest. Providing an answer to a problem the research community has already been interested in is in most instances much more valuable than a coordinated fishing expedition. Reverse engineering from empirical patterns in the data often leads into ex-ante much less interesting theoretical territory. The fit between empirics and theory the p-hackers unearth may shed light on theoretical topics that are of only little interest to the research community. In fact, in economics it is rather unlikely that a pure data-driven search will generate major scientific discoveries we have not already been aware of in some form. Even though reverse engineering may open up interesting new avenues, the majority of reverse engineered studies will show all sorts of less relevant and comparatively weak discoveries.

Moreover, if the theoretical arguments in a study are inconsistent or incoherent, the study is likely to have been the result of badly executed reverse engineering. Reverse engineering can only be successful if the distilled empirical evidence also matches reasonably with the proposed theory. If p-hackers detect some very unusual statistical associations, they will not be able to find a good theory in the literature supporting them and instead will resort to ad-hoc theorizing, plastered together from various sources. Experienced economists can easily spot and dissect such a "theory". If the theoretical setup of the study seems rather messy, the study was probably subject to reverse engineering.

Bettis (2012) describes how theories erected on false feedback can lead to disorder in the literature.

> In many cases, once such a significant coefficient is found, the theory being tested is metaphorically hoisted up to the appropriate place in the theoretical superstructure of the field and firmly welded into the "gap" between other "proven" hypotheses for which significant coefficients have previously been found. There it subsequently provides connections onto which further theoretical beams can be welded as appropriate hypotheses are developed and tested. This is the way that at least some of what we consider theory is built today, one or a few significant coefficients at a time. Given the problems with repeated tests, I worry that some, and perhaps a lot, of the theory we are building may be more like a house of cards than a strong and enduring edifice of tightly welded steel beams.

One might ask whether p-hacking indeed has the power to detect real patterns in the data or whether it merely leads to manifestations of the "infinite monkey theorem". The infinite monkey theorem states that a monkey hitting on a typewriter for an infinite amount of time will eventually write any sort of text, like, for instance, the collected works of Shakespeare. This metaphor implies that researchers mining their data very extensively will eventually uncover all sorts of statistical patterns.

The success of a p-hacker therefore hinges critically on his or her ability to determine whether the detected patterns are indeed plausible and theoretically relevant. Successful p-hackers disregard the majority of their discovered findings, because they understand that they are just statistical noise. This constant evaluation of the value of alternative statistical findings is in fact the most difficult aspect of p-hacking. Successfully p-hacking can feel like a key that finally fits the lock. The distilled match between theory and results seems so perfect that it simply has to be true.

Experienced researchers are often able to create elegant matches between the discovered empirical evidence and the reverse engineered theories. If they corrected their repeatedly executed estimations adequately for multiple comparisons, could their robust p-hacking then maybe even lead to the true feedback we so dearly seek? Unfortunately, this is largely an illusion. Whereas robust p-hacking allows uncovering formidable matches between theoretical arguments and empirical evidence, it does no better in mapping these matches than any ex-ante approach. The robustly p-hacked and then reverse engineered empirical evidence is even likely to be a worse representation of the theoretical arguments, as the researchers are often guided by statistical significance, and less by ex-ante thoughts about the optimal way through the garden of forking paths.

Data-driven theory formulation suffers from exactly the same problems caused by the wide garden of forking paths. The whole problem is just flipped on its head; p-hackers walk their way through the garden of forking paths backward. They face the same trade-offs with respect to all their decisions as if they were developing their entire theory from an ex-ante perspective; the inductive decisions will be loaded with ambiguous trade-offs. No p-hacked empirical evidence allows to unambiguously uncover true theoretical arguments. P-hackers do not know whether the final econometric model they obtained is in true correspondence to the theoretical arguments they formulated. Testing a theory necessitates following a true way through the garden of forking paths, and the p-hacked, most significant or most robust econometric model is not said to correspond to such a true way. For example, the p-hacked econometric model may lack some not obvious but crucial covariates, which could have been discovered through a sophisticated ex-ante investigation. The inevitable result of data-driven theory formulation is false feedback. Moreover, different researchers will naturally end up with different matches between theoretical arguments and empirical evidence. P-hacking thus produces false feedback by allocating false theoretical arguments to the carefully distilled empirical evidence.

While the decisions along an ex-ante way through the garden of forking paths correspond to a series of forking paths from theory to empirics, p-hacking applied to detect patterns in the data corresponds to a series of forking paths from empirics to theory. Both times researchers need to choose their path in the face of numerous alternative forks, without there being an unambiguously true path. Every fork in the garden is shadowed by at least some vagueness. The difference between the two ways to approach research is that in the first instant theory is the leader, while in the second instant empirics is the leader. In both cases we inevitably observe a relationship between theory and empirics characterized by false feedback, although arguably likely less so if theory has been the leader.

In fact, there also exist statistical methods explicitly designed for the pursuit of data mining (i.e., robust p-hacking). Given that the search space incorporates the true econometric model, these methods would be able to filter it out. Prominent examples of such methods are model averaging (Sala-i-Martin 1997), multiple hypotheses testing frameworks (White 2000), or the general-to-simple model selection (GETS) (Hoover and Perez 2004). However, all of these alternative statistical methods are restricted to the choice between explanatory variables. Moreover, in practice, the true econometric model is seldom part of the search space.

Finally, even if the p-hacking has been accounted for and the detected pattern is real and not merely a statistical fluke, the reverse engineered theory did still not pass attempts at falsification. If a researcher builds a theory on a set of facts, these facts cannot themselves refute the theory. A theory can only be falsified through the prediction of new facts; only if the theory aligns with these novel predictions, it has stood up to attempts at falsification. Otherwise, although the theory might seem to fit the detected pattern perfectly, the theory may still be false, as it could miss out on central factors that overturn its very core. Thus, reverse engineering from data to theory can create elegant matches that are still false. If empirical aspects are not present in the data at hand, the theory will miss out on them, and only new data can then show the actual merits of the theory.

6.6 Biased estimates versus false positives

False feedback can take on two forms: a) biased estimates and b) false positives. An estimate is biased when its expected value deviates from the true value of the underlying effect. This occurs when the underlying variable is endogenous, because of, for example, omitted variable bias or reverse causality. In contrast, false positives are caused through statistical noise. The estimate itself may well be unbiased, meaning that it would, in expectation, converge toward the true effect. However, the data have fallen (or been p-hacked) in such a way that the estimate deviates from the true effect. Hence, while endogeneity is the cause behind biased estimates, statistical noise is the cause behind false positives. Biased estimates are both real and replicable; if the same analysis would be repeated on different datasets, we would again observe the same biased estimates (Simonsohn et al. 2019). In contrast, false positives are neither real nor replicable, since they would evaporate if the same analysis would be repeated on different datasets (Simonsohn et al. 2019), that is, they are mere statistical flukes.

Observational studies can usually profit from larger sample sizes and thus face fewer false positives but face challenges in eliminating all possible sources of bias in the estimated effects. Experimental studies, in contrast, usually face less challenges in the form of bias but, due to their smaller sample sizes, are more harmed by false positives, especially when coupled with p-hacking (Gelman and Carlin 2014). In general, observational studies produce more false feedback in the form of biased estimates, whereas experimental studies produce more false feedback in the form of false positives.

Experiments with a very simple setup, such as certain laboratory experiments in behavioral economics, are often able to approach the true way through the garden of forking path quite well. Since they rely on fewer and more transparent auxiliary hypotheses, they face good odds at indeed uncovering true feedback. If, however, researchers p-hack their data, experiments can nevertheless produce false feedback. While, in expectation, the experiments may indeed deliver unbiased estimates, the molding of the applied specifications onto statistical noise vastly increases the chances of obtaining false positives. Thus, while very simple experiments are comparatively free from concerns about biased estimates, even modest p-hacking can increase the number of false positives.

Take, for instance, the infamous article of Bem (2011) about "feeling the future". In this article, Bem (2011) presents nine experiments, involving more than 1000 participants, to show the existence of psi. Eight out of nine experiments show statistically significant "evidence" that future causal events (images) have an influence on individuals' past responses. For these experiments to be true, almost everything we currently understand about the natural sciences must be false. Hence, the natural conclusion about Bem's (2011) study is that these experiments must show false positives, even though they seem executed perfectly by the standards of the top journal in psychology it was published in.

In observational studies, p-hacking does seldom only lead to false positives but causes biased estimates, too. In their search for statistical significance, p-hackers do not just vary those researcher degrees of freedom that remain inconsequential for potential endogeneity but always vary at least some researcher degrees of freedom that also cause bias to the estimates. Hence, alternating researcher degrees of freedom in an observational study causes variation in false feedback that originates from both biased estimates and false positives. The fact that the two sources of false feedback interact with each other makes matters even worse. In observational studies searching for statistical significance therefore capitalizes not just on statistical noise but also on endogeneity.

For example, in a well-conducted experiment, alternating covariates to find statistical significance can at most leverage on statistical noise. In contrast, in an observational study, covariates can leverage on statistical noise *and* on sources of endogeneity like omitted variable bias. Thus, the chances to "discover" a statistically significant estimate are higher in observational studies, as the researchers can profit from two distinct sources when varying the available degrees of freedom.

6.7 Self-deception and deception of others

Most researchers think that their p-hacking is not an issue because they firmly believe in the research ideas they have developed. After working on a project for a long time, researchers naturally start to believe in it. Turning around arguments in your head for such a long time leads you into thinking that the drawn conclusions must indeed also be true. Constant repetition of a message weakens even the smartest and most reflective minds. Many researchers also see their alleged scientific discoveries as their personal intellectual offspring. They therefore have a tendency to think that their p-hacking is not a problem because it only supports a true conclusion which anyway corresponds to reality.

Even for reflective researchers it always takes a mental effort to not fall prey to self-deception and to not just opt for those researcher degrees of freedom that show more favorable results instead of explicitly choosing the researcher degrees of freedom that are more appropriate, especially when the latter set of researcher degrees of freedom is not very obviously more adequate. If, for example, researchers are ambiguous about the exact way how to operationalize a theoretical concept, and then see in the data that one of the constructed variables fits their story much better, they will instantly start to think about good reasons why this particular operationalization should be chosen, and good reasons why the other possible operationalizations could be more problematic.

The most self-deceptive researchers also tend to think that when the statistical program produced a certain result, they have done nothing wrong and that they certainly did not deceive anyone about the obtained findings. They pick their preferred model specification and believe that, because the statistical program calculated it, the results must at least somehow be true, as raw numbers donot lie. This is why adequate graphical analysis of the data is so important. It is in almost all cases the most transparent way to pursue in applied research. A set of informative plots about the investigated relationships allows judgment about whether we are moving in the right direction or not, and whether we have indeed uncovered statistical associations exhibiting substance. Otherwise, the entire empirical analysis runs the risk of being a black box thriving on statistical artefacts, since most statistical estimators are blind to the actual distribution of the data (see, e.g., Anscombe's quartette).

The reason why p-hacking has become so pervasive in economics is certainly the low computing costs. In modern econometric software packages, most estimations run through in only a few seconds, making it possible to try out a huge number of different estimations. Thus, with respect to p-hacking, well-designed older empirical studies may be more reliable than more recent empirical studies. Seventy years ago, the high cost of computation enabled researchers to run at most a few different estimations (e.g., matrices had to be inverted by hand). This one-shot statistical testing forced researcher to fully think through an ex-ante appropriate statistical model.

P-hacking also undermines basic principles of thinking about statistics. Every applied economist knows that, all else equal, the smaller the sample size, the more the respective estimates will vary. If, however, contrary to our expectations, we still find a statistically significant estimate in a small sample, then this will constitute even stronger evidence against the null hypothesis, because we have pursued an especially demanding test. The hypothesized effect should be even more likely to be present because we were able to detect it against the background of substantial statistical noise. However, Gelman and Carlin (2014) show that when the true effect sizes are small and researchers screen for statistical significance, the corresponding estimates can be hugely overblown or even move into the wrong direction. If the power with respect to the (small) true effect is 80%, this will not be an issue. If, however, the power is less than 0.5, researchers will start to observe statistically significant effects that can be many times larger than the true effect sizes (Type M errors). If the power is less than 0.1, they will even start to observe statistically significant effects with the wrong sign (Type S errors). The option to selectively report only statistically significant estimates completely undermines the fact that low p-values are harder to obtain in small samples. If researchers pursue intense p-hacking, they will "discover" sufficient interesting Type M or even Type S errors that will allow publishing well.

To obtain numbers on how pervasive p-hacking indeed is remains difficult. We have some indications from the field of psychology, for instance. John et al. (2012) conducted an anonymous online survey among over 2000 academic psychologists at major U.S. universities to elicit whether they had engaged in questionable research practices such as p-hacking. For example, nearly 50% of the participants stated that, in a study, they had selectively reported only studies that "work". To correct for the fact that survey participants tend to underreport socially undesirable practices, John et al. (2012) also included questions where participants could provide estimates of what they thought was the behavior of other academic psychologist. When combined with these latter judgments, the percentage of psychologists that engaged in questionable research practices rose substantially; for example, the declared rate of survey participants who selectively reported studies that work increased to 67%.

Necker (2014) presents similar numbers as John et al. (2012) for a sample of professional, mostly academic economists. Her data stem from an anonymous online survey among 2520 members of the European Economic Association (EEA), which was completed by 426 respondents (a response rate of 16.9%). 93.7% of the surveyed economists engaged in at least one questionable research practice, which is almost the same as the number of 94% in John et al. (2012). The answers regarding the individual practices differed substantially, however. Only about 3% of survey participants reported to have fabricated data, whereas about 35% reported practices related to p-hacking, such as searching for control variables until one gets the desired result. These estimates constitute only a lower boundary though, as admitting to questionable research practices suffers from social desirability bias, or even a fear to get caught. Estimates about the prevalence of questionable research practices among other researchers, as in John et al. (2012), are probably more reliable in this respect.

To obtain an idea of how common questionable research practices are, we can also rely on testimonies from individual researchers. Unfortunately, because of a (justified) fear of retaliation, these whistle blowers usually want to remain anonymous. No researcher wants to be publicly called out for the use of questionable research practices, whether they have been pursued intentionally or not. Gelman (2020) cites the testimony from an anonymous graduate student in economics at a European university, who has worked several years as a research assistant and sometimes as a coauthor with multiple different professors and senior researchers. He reports that,

> In my experience, all social science researchers that I have worked with seem to treat the process of writing a paper as some kind of exercise in going "back-and-forth" between theoretical analysis and empirical evidence. Just as an example, they (we) might run X number of regressions, and try to find a fitting theory that can explain the results. Researchers with the most top publications often seem to get/have access to the greatest number of RAs and PhD students, who perform thousands of analyses that only very few people will ever hear about unless something "promising" is found (or unless you happen to share the same office). I have performed plenty of such analyses myself.

One might rightfully ask how many more other graduate students experience the very same issues as this anonymous graduate student.

We have not discussed the issue of misconduct in academics so far. It is an open secret that from time to time some of the most opportunistic researchers fake their statistical results in order to be able to publish well, because they think that otherwise they cannot survive in the highly competitive academic system. An extreme example is the study of LaCour and Green (2014) about the transmission of support for gay equality, which was published in the prestigious journal "Science", but retracted after about a year because of serious allegations of misconduct. It turned out that LaCour, then a graduate student in political sciences at Columbia University, fabricated his entire dataset. This instance of large-scale fabrication of data raises the question of how much other misconduct we may be missing out. To get a general idea of scientific misconduct, one can just browse on "Retraction Watch" (2020). However, those are again almost always very obvious cases that were comparatively easy to discover. There are certainly many small instances of misconduct in research we will never know about.

6.8 Abandon statistical significance?

As discussed in Section 6.1, the American Statistical Association, among others, has called for an abandonment of the use of p-values to decide whether an empirical result is useful or not (Wasserstein and Lazar 2016). This appeal has been a reaction to the frequent misuse of p-values in the biomedical and social sciences, where authors often make scientific conclusions mainly based on whether a p-value has crossed the 0.05 threshold or not (McShane et al. 2019a). Wasserstein et al. (2019) state that "no p-value can reveal the plausibility, presence, truth, or importance of an association or effect". Wasserstein and Lazar (2016) argue that the use of continuous p-values is fine, as long as they are not used as a decision criterion about which results to show in the study. The focus needs to be on the context of the study and not on the p-values. They further argue that we need to accept uncertainty about statistical effects and break with the false certainty promised by statistical significance. The fact that we cannot make a precise statement is by itself already valuable information. Wasserstein and Lazar (2016) argue that a shift away from statistical significance thresholds will enable a focus on better measures, more sensitive design, and better execution, which would increase the rigor of research.

Statistical significance has lost much of its value over time because it stopped being an aid to judge the merit of a study and instead became a target itself. Because statistical significance is necessary for publication, researchers found ways to meet it regardless of the factual basis.

In contrast, Ioannidis (2019) argues that in a world without statistical significance anyone could claim any effect to be relevant. Removing barriers to decide whether a study provides useful evidence or not may encourage researchers to overstretch their results even more. The tendency to exaggerate one's own findings will not disappear, since it does not remove the incentives of researchers to present evidence in favor of a publishable discovery. Researchers may indeed cut their efforts to pursue p-hacking, but instead focus on other aspects of the data that favor their respective cases. Ioannidis (2019) even argues that abandoning statistical significance would lead to "statistical anarchy", because researcher could "rely less on data and evidence and more on subjective opinions and interpretations".

A group of 72 researchers has thus proposed to change the p-value threshold for statistical significance of 0.05 in fields where it is common to a lower threshold of only 0.005 (Benjamin et al. 2018). They apply Bayesian reasoning and evidence from replication projects to arrive at this 0.005 significance threshold. Benjamin et al. (2018) argue that this step would immediately increase the replicability rate. Results crossing only the 0.05 threshold should instead be termed as "suggestive". A transition toward a 0.005 threshold is simple and could quickly gain acceptance among the research community (Benjamin et al. 2018). It would require about 70% larger sample sizes to maintain a power of 80% though, which means that, given current budgets, fewer studies could be pursued. However, Benjamin et al. (2018) show that false-positive rates would fall by more than a factor of two, which would save costs for expensive follow-up studies building on false positives. The efficiency gain would thus outweigh the losses. Importantly, Benjamin et al. (2018) argue that their proposal should not be used to reject publications of findings that only fall below a p-value threshold of 0.05. Selection should rather be on motivation of the research question and on the quality of the research methods.

Nonetheless, Ioannidis (2018a) argues that lowering the p-value threshold to 0.005 is only a temporizing measure. It would "work as a dam that could help gain time and prevent drowning by a flood statistical significance". In the meantime, we should seek more durable solutions. Ioannidis (2018a) argues that this may involve abandoning statistical significance thresholds entirely. Moreover, a p-value threshold of 0.005 may in fact increase false feedback if researchers resort to bending their results even more to obtain statistical significance. In the long run, we would have to focus on, for instance, effect sizes and their uncertainty, without any adherence to strict thresholds for statistical significance (Ioannidis 2018a). The research methods should take center stage and not the p-value.

A study that shows statistically insignificant results should be published if the very same study would have been published had it shown statistically significant results. Consequently, case-by-case judgment of studies is preferable to adherence to arbitrary decision criteria like thresholds of statistical significance. In contrast to p-hacking, overemphasizing of results in the published article is at least transparent in the published article itself; it signals the high uncertainty inherent to the statistical analysis and does not hide as near certainty behind low p-values crossing specific significance threshold.

At least partial relief for the search for statistical significance could come from a somewhat unexpected side: the digital revolution. With life taking place more and more online, and the corresponding constant tracking of all our online activities, we now have numerous very large datasets with millions of observations available, where every single coefficient in the statistical model will turn out statistically significant. Researchers will thus not anymore be forced to search for specifications that fall below some (implicit) p-value threshold. This would free up capacity and allow instead an increased focus on the adequacy of all the separate methodological decisions.

The fact that in very large datasets all coefficients are statistically significant will shift the attention toward their economic significance (McCloskey and Ziliak 1996, 2004). If the thresholds for the occurrence of type I errors are fixed, increasing the sample size lowers the occurrence of type II errors. With a large enough sample size, even very small effects will be detected as statistically significant. The null hypothesis of no effect is seldom true; most variables correlate at least a somewhat with each other. Very large datasets will require researchers to discuss the size of their obtained coefficients.

Some effects can be difficult to estimate even within large samples though, since the variation necessary to identify the effects of interest can still be small. This can happen, for example, when the exogenous variation extracted through the identification strategy is not sufficient to deliver a statistically significant estimate. Estimates in large samples can therefore suffer from the very same problem as estimates in small samples. The sample size alone is sometimes not sufficient to provide the necessary power. A large sample size alone cannot guarantee to not hit upon false negatives.

Moreover, in economics, the size of many datasets will always be restricted by the fact that the studied settings have only so and so many firms, workers, countries, etc. Data generated through digital transactions cannot resolve issues about the size of the underlying population.

Very large datasets also do not alter the possibility of hacking the statistical findings toward stronger evidence in line with the ex-ante defined theoretical arguments. While they free researchers from the search for statistical significance, they do not prohibit the possibility that researchers use their degrees of freedom to make the variables of interest more economically significant. The larger the coefficients, the bigger the story (as long as they stay within the "credible range"). The reason for this behavior is, once again, that, except in those rare cases, where they contradict some widely accepted theory, publishing null results remains seldom possible, even if coupled with very small standard errors. Unfortunately, even if direly needed, falsifications are seldom welcome in economics.

Nonetheless, since large samples are generally less affected by statistical noise, a given route through the garden of forking paths will deliver more stable feedback. The feedback may still be false, but it will change much less between different datasets. This stability of results could lead to the problem that, even if the feedback is far from true feedback, the repeated instances of the same false feedback may give the wrong impression that we have hit on true feedback. However, the relevance of questions about the adequacy of methodological decisions will necessarily become more apparent, because researchers will perceive how changes in specific researcher degrees of freedom can lead to very different results, even though the results remain statistically significant. They cannot get around realizing that statistical significance by itself does not guarantee true feedback. If the seal of approval by statistical significance becomes irrelevant, the focus of the researchers will directly shift to whether they have indeed chosen the right ways through their respective garden of forking paths.

Consequently, the gold standard in empirical research should not just be RCTs, but straightforward RCTs with very high statistical power. Simplicity of the research design reduces the problems of identifying the true way through the garden of forking paths, and, equally important, offers less room for hacking the obtained estimates into a specific direction. High statistical power will further make the hunting of statistical significance superfluous. The only critical aspect in such a highly powered study is the effect size, which will be harder to manipulate the more straightforward the RCTS is.

Notes

1 Whether a researcher drops an unsuccessful project probably depends a lot on his or her ability to recognize a potential "failure" early on, and, importantly, on his or her necessity to publish studies. An assistant professor up for tenure cannot let project after project go, as he or she has to finish at least some of them. Moreover, the success of a project also embodies the problem of luck in research. Many researchers have good ideas, which ex-ante can all seem very reasonable, while, unfortunately, only some of them will work out when put to the test.
2 The Benjamini and Hochberg method first sorts the p-values in ascending order, in a so-called linear step-up procedure. It then looks for the first "k" p-values that cross the threshold $p(i) <= i/m*q$, where "i" is the rank of the respective p-value "p(i)", "m" is the number of hypotheses tested, and "q" is the FDR, that is, the expected proportion of false discoveries we would like to have (e.g., 0.05). It rejects all hypotheses h(i) for which "i" is an element in (1,2,3,...,k). For instance, if a researcher runs 100 trials, and 30 out of those trials are statistically significant, while only 10 are highly significant and 20 are marginally significant, the latter 20 trials will not cross the conservative threshold of $a=1-(1-f)^{1/c}$ of the Šidàk correction. In contrast, the FDR will reject up to the first p-value "k" that crosses the boundary $p(i)<=i/m*q$, which can be considerably more instances than in the case of the Šidàk correction, especially if numerous hypotheses are tested, as the gain in power of the Benjamini and Hochberg method increases in the number of tested hypotheses. Benjamini and Hochberg (2001) show that their method is also valid for most structures of dependence between tests most relevant for empirical analysis.

7 The illusion of true feedback

In Chapter 1, we defined false feedback as false empirical results that take on the appearance of true empirical results. The process of mistaking false feedback for true feedback gives rise to an "illusion of true feedback". Well-published studies in economics have an inherent tendency to appear true to other researchers. Their polished structure suggests a false exactness of the world by implying that everything is ordered and precise, and one can easily forget about the vast garden of forking paths.

The economic literature certainly contains numerous studies approximating true feedback quite well. However, and this is the problem for all of empirical economics, they are difficult to spot. They do usually not stand out prominently among the mass of all other seemingly true studies. False feedback may be easier to identify in publications in more obscure journals, as they sometimes make decisions in the garden of forking paths that are evidently wrong. In contrast, the majority of studies published in top journals appear like unambiguous true feedback. They navigate the garden of forking paths seemingly very well, and only few of their problems show themselves openly to other researchers.

For instance, when evaluating a published study, you may argue that it suffers from specific problems of endogeneity. However, you never know how large this concern actually looms. The study could still be closer to true feedback than another study with a seemingly cleaner identification strategy. If you read a published study, endogeneity remains invisible, you can only argue that it is there, but you cannot know its extent. It may loom both larger or smaller than we may think.

The Greek philosopher Xenophanes (around 580–500 BC) argued that even if we are lucky enough to believe the truth, we cannot be certain whether our beliefs have indeed hit the truth. We cannot know whether we know the truth about the nature of things. Xenophanes was thus one of the earliest advocates of the separation of knowledge from true belief. We can have true beliefs about the nature of all things, but this would be more of a coincidence, since we lack sufficient reason to be certain that these beliefs are indeed true. Similarly, if we rely on published empirical studies, we will often hit on true feedback, but we will have limited ways of knowing whether these studies indeed correspond to true feedback.

In an analogy taken from Leamer (1983), the illusion of true feedback is akin to the manufacturing of sausages in a factory. Econometric estimation, just like the sausage factory, always produces properly looking, neat results. The estimated parameters seem plausible, just as the manufactured sausages tend to look tasty. The problem arises only when eating a sausage made of bad ingredients, or when relying on an econometric result based on false assumptions. Both can generally not be judged by their appearance; for this, close inspection of the ingredients of the sausage or of the model assumptions would be necessary. While this is easy with sausages, it is hard with econometric results.

Since the critique of Leamer (1983), there has been substantial development in empirical methods though. Most important here is probably the focus on causal research designs in the spirit of Angrist and Pischke (2008). Yet while causal research designs have indeed greatly reduced false feedback, they could not eliminate it. Causal research designs focus on the validity of a certain aspect in the econometric model, such as the exclusion restriction in an instrumental variable approach, parallel pre-trends in a difference-in-differences setting, or the absence of strategic action around the cutoff in a regression discontinuity design. Whereas simple correlational analyses often do not provide convincing ways to assess whether we have hit on true feedback or not, causal research designs put us with their focus on key aspects of the econometric model into the right direction. Good causal research designs center the econometric model around true feedback and therefore at least allow us a shot at uncovering it. Nonetheless, causal research designs are no less silent about numerous choices in the garden of forking paths than simple correlational analyses. As we have laid out in the previous chapter, these choices can be severe sources of false feedback, too. Even if good causal research designs allow centering in on true feedback, they still remain subject to heavy variation around it.

Ironically, in their search for causal estimates, some researchers actually increase the false feedback produced by their econometric models. For example, when they force their data into a causal research design for which the circumstances are clearly not appropriate. Causal research designs may in such unfortunate instances even be less appropriate than simple correlational analyses, leading to more and not less false feedback. For example, when in a difference-in-differences design the setup is twisted too much in order to provide evidence in line with parallel pre-trends. In fact, enforcing parallel pre-trends is akin to the enforcing of statistical significance. Just as we would expect to regularly observe statistically insignificant results, we should at least in some settings observe deviations from parallel pre-trends. However, nearly all published difference-in-differences studies do show parallel pre-trends. This implies that researchers either resort to the file drawer, or, more likely, actively search for parallel pre-trends. Another example for when causal research designs can in fact worsen things is the well-known problem of weak instrumental variables, where the instrument may indeed be exogenous but only moderately correlated with the endogenous variable. Weak instruments seem to be much more pervasive in economics than we might think (see, e.g., Young 2019). They can make matters worse and even cause an increase in false feedback when compared to uncorrected OLS. While everyone knows that a simple correlational analysis is seldom causal, most researchers are convinced that, if only they apply a causal research design, their results will by definition turn out to be causal, too, even if they rely on rather shaky assumptions. Unfortunately, the spread of causal research designs has eroded much of the skepticism researchers should have toward their own results.

Experienced researchers are often better able to order different research studies according to their quality. Some studies are quite visibly closer to or further away from true feedback than others. However, the problem resurfaces in full force if one compares two conflicting studies that both use a seemingly well-specified and clean identification strategy; in such cases, decision making becomes arbitrary again. Unfortunately, high-quality studies do not contradict each other less often than low-quality studies. A researcher involved as an author in two articles could make an adequate judgment about their approximate truth values. Yet as a mere observer, such judgment is very difficult. In practice, most researchers just use the credentials of the authors as a heuristic for its truth value.

In fact, it does not matter that much whether some skilled researchers are indeed able to adequately weigh two well-conducted but contradictory studies against each other in a more objective way, because the large majority of researchers cannot, myself included. Since all of these researchers actively contribute studies to the literature, too, it becomes very difficult to order studies.

Even the most accomplished scientists can be fooled by the illusion of true feedback. In his book "Thinking Fast and Slow" Nobel laureate Daniel Kahneman (2011) writes about social priming in psychology that "disbelief is not an option. The results are not made up, nor are they statistical flukes. You have no choice but to accept that the major conclusions of these studies are true". He dedicates a whole chapter to social priming in his book, with studies such as Bargh (1996), who primed college students in a task to assemble sentences with words related to old age such as "Florida", "forgetful", "bald", "gray", or "wrinkle". After the students had completed the task, they had to move to a different room to complete a different task. The researchers measured the time the students took to walk to this next room and "found" that the primed students walked significantly slower than the nonprimed students, just like old people would do. However, soon after the publication of Kahneman's book in 2011, reports started to come out that failed to replicate major studies in social priming. Kahneman himself quickly realized that a train wreck was looming in social priming research (Schimmack et al. 2017). Unfortunately, his prediction came true, and most major studies in social priming failed to replicate (see, e.g., Open Science Collaboration 2015). Kahneman himself should have known better from the outset though, since 11 of the 12 social priming studies described in his 2011 book were severely underpowered (Schimmack et al. 2017). Tversky and Kahneman (1971) wrote in their article entitled "belief in the law of small numbers" that scientists can have an "exaggerated confidence in the validity of conclusions based on small samples". In this article, they argue that researchers regularly overestimate the probability of rejecting the null hypothesis in small samples and, as a consequence, most studies in psychology are underpowered. However, Kahneman was obviously not puzzled by the simultaneous observation that studies in psychology, nonetheless, almost always deliver statistically significant results. These two scenarios are clearly mutually exclusive. One cannot have a series of underpowered studies that, nevertheless, almost always show statistically significant estimates. At least some of them should remain insignificant. When even a scientist of the standing of Kahneman can suffer from the illusion of true feedback, almost none of us will be exempt from it. Given the fierce resistance many researchers in social priming have shown during the replication crisis, it seems that even those researchers who are themselves executing false studies may not realize that they thrive on false feedback. They very obviously believe in the false feedback they have produced.

Schimmack (2012) describes the adverse effect that presenting many statistically significant results can have on the credibility of an article. In psychology, for instance, researchers often present multiple studies within a single article, which together should provide stronger support for the underlying theory. However, in case the individual studies are underpowered, at least some of them should turn up statistically insignificant. For instance, if the power of each study is only 50%, and ten out of ten studies nevertheless show statistically significant results, the probability of this occurrence is less than 0.0009 (=0.5^{10}). Schimmack (2012) argues that an article showing only statistically significant results may, in fact, be less credible than articles showing mixed results, as the researchers probably resorted to the use of practices like p-hacking. With only moderate power, too many statistically significant results within a single article can weaken rather than strengthen the confidence in the article.

Many researchers tend to ignore the difficulties arising from researcher degrees of freedom because they argue that the literature as a whole will in any case after some time converge to a clear picture into a specific direction, rendering such methodological details irrelevant. However, social priming research was a whole literature, and based on a large variety of experiments, which we consider the gold standard of clean identification and many think that few things can go wrong.

The perception of how biased an estimate in a published study is also depends strongly on your prior beliefs about the direction and size of the underlying effect. If a study publishes a large positive estimate that according to your own priors should have been near zero or even negative, concerns about potential bias, which in other, similar settings you would probably have deemed as inconsequential, will suddenly appear as very relevant to you.

Most problematic are those researchers who doubt all published studies that falsify their own beliefs but, in contrast, trust all those published studies that confirm their own beliefs, while both times ignoring whether the respective studies indeed approximate true feedback or not.

Too many researchers thus act inversely to everything Karl Popper stood for. They rely on their existing beliefs and search for evidence that confirms these beliefs. If in the process they hit on facts that might contradict these beliefs, they simply ignore them and instead focus on only those alternative facts that support their beliefs. Such a strategy will never let you make any intellectual progress, as you will always find some evidence that aligns with your prior beliefs. The tendency to search for confirmatory evidence and to neglect contradictory evidence is a well-known phenomenon, not only in science but everywhere, and is called "confirmation bias" (Nickerson 1998).

The large variation in findings of empirical studies in economics amplifies the problem of confirmation bias, since researchers with strong prior beliefs on a certain subject will always find at least some studies that seem to support their initial positions. Without a culture that sets a systematic emphasis on the reliability of empirical findings, too many researchers will continue to rely selectively on only those studies that favor their own beliefs.

To expose false certainty, it is sufficient to increase the stakes (Popper 1972). For example, you may have the feeling that quite a few of your beliefs are true with certainty. However, if the stakes involved increase, you start to realize that you are actually not that certain about almost all of them. If your life depends on the truth of a given belief, you will start to endlessly double-check everything in order for it to indeed be true.

Many of the studies best approximating true feedback are also published in lower-ranked journals, where, unfortunately, they are often ignored, since they have a tendency to seem less true. They do not profit from the superior aesthetics of studies published in top journals, with their nice formulas, their nice editing, and their nice writing style, which together cover up all kinds of potential shortfalls. An excellent write-up of an academic article can hide much of its actual weakness.

Brodeur et al. (2020) find that top 5 journals are no better with respect to p-hacking than non-top 5 journals, as they both show the same two-humped or camel-shaped distribution of test statistics. Importantly, Brodeur et al. (2020) also show that there is no evidence that the revise and resubmit process mitigates the problem of p-hacking. Working papers show similar distributions of test statistics as the published versions of the articles.

Moreover, despite the increasing awareness, p-hacking as identified by Brodeur et al. (2020) has also not visibly improved over the last decade.

The problem in economics is that we cannot verify most auxiliary hypotheses. Mayo (1996b) argues that in an experiment the target should always be to rule out the presence of false auxiliary hypotheses. This would then allow severe, or precise, tests of hypotheses. In the natural sciences, this means checking all the experimental apparatuses, in a piecemeal fashion, just like in any other practical tasks. Unfortunately, in economics, knowledge of the falsity of auxiliary hypotheses in the setup of a given study is in most instances impossible. The true statistical model remains invisible. For instance, how can we know whether our models include all relevant explanatory variables? Such auxiliary hypotheses remain elusive and can thus not be definitely judged as true or false. For many important auxiliary hypotheses we have no other choice than merely to assume them as true. The illusion of true feedback emerges precisely when such assumptions are false but cannot be recognized as such.

Because they have realized that broad claims about the causality of their estimates are insufficient, applied researcher nowadays set a strong emphasis on key identifying assumptions. One cannot simply assume causality anymore but has to support the key identifying assumptions with good reasons. Before the credibility revolution, researchers just had to indicate that their estimates are not endogenous via, for example, variation in model specifications. The burden of proof on whether an estimate is endogenous or not was on the reader. Nowadays, researchers are required to explicitly show that their findings are causal, that they result from exogenous variation. In a natural experiment, for example, the researchers need to explain in detail why their treatment should be as good as randomly allocated. The burden of proof is now on the researchers, who have to show that their estimates are free from concerns of endogeneity.

However, while the focus on key identifying assumptions has increased, and thus moved us closer to true feedback, the focus on other auxiliary hypotheses has decreased, and moved us further away from true feedback again. It is not so much endogenous setups anymore that cause the false feedback in our studies, but this latter set of auxiliary hypotheses, the vast garden of forking paths.

8 False feedback bubbles

The common sense view of scientific progress portrays knowledge as cumulative. It regards each study as a separate finding that is either true or false. Once published, each study stands by itself as an additional contribution to the literature. The studies are then either trustworthy, meaning that they can be independently replicated, or not (see, e.g., Grimes et al. 2018). Scientific progress is thus portrayed as an increase in the proportion of correct findings. Each study is seen as an independent discovery, and the question whether there is scientific progress depends on what proportion of this body of scientific evidence is correct or not (see, e.g., Ioannidis 2012). Over time, the self-correcting nature of science would then weed out false feedback. Ioannidis (2012) argues that the proper working of this self-correcting mechanism is often questionable though; false feedback may perpetuate itself, or morph into alternative, equally or even more false versions of empirical feedback.

Yet the target of science is not the production of isolated facts but of theories able to explain these facts and thus our reality. Popper (1972) argues that scientific knowledge develops revolutionary; theories do not build on each other but rather replace each other. Through trial and error, theories fit reality better and better over time, which is the scientific progress we observe. The interaction with reality, in the form of empirical testing, uncovers errors in our theories and provides the basis for the development of better theories. The falsification of a core hypothesis of a theory can give valuable hints at how entirely new economic theories, which are able to account for it, must look like. The newly developed theories are then empirically tested again, with theories improving more and more over time. Popper (1985) argues that "The evolution of scientific knowledge is, in the main, the evolution of better and better theories. The theories become better adapted through natural selection: they give us better information about reality". The crucial aspect is the replacement of existing theories with competing theories that have a higher truth content. The growth of scientific knowledge is one of error elimination; it is a process of Darwinian selection.

In his book "Objective knowledge", Popper (1972) introduces what he calls the "third world", which is the universe of problems, conjectures, theories, critical arguments, and the content of journals, books, and libraries. It is "largely autonomous, even though we constantly act upon it and are acted upon by it: it is autonomous in spite of the fact that it is our product and that is has a strong feedback effect on us". Popper (1972) argues that the objects of the third world exist independently of the human mind. Human minds create theories and are, in turn, influenced by them, but theories have their own existence as objects with the potential to be discovered. Popper (1972) argues that science makes progress through the feedback we obtain from this third world. Theories provide their feedback to us in the form of the errors we uncover through critical discussion, which we, in turn, can use for improving the theories. However, the problem with Popper's third world is that it also contains false theories and everything in between true and false theories. Unlike the physical world, we do not get feedback from what really is, namely solely from true theories, but also from false theories. The feedback we obtain can therefore be very misleading. The idea that the third world also contains falsity poses a problem to the growth of knowledge. Without a proper anchor setting a standard for evaluation we cannot make progress. Popper (1972) assumes that our critical arguments play this role. However, and this is the main thesis of the book, in many settings, our critical arguments do not approach truth much better than the theories themselves, as they are based on facts that are uncertain, too.

Truth can play its role as a regulator only if we can assure that our critical arguments correspond to the facts. Otherwise, it cannot adequately judge our pursuit of knowledge, that is, whether we found a theory that passes our tests or not. Rational criticism is only an instrument but not itself an anchor able to assure that we are on the right track. If we do not know whether our theories fall short of truth or not, whether there are even any problems after all, rational criticism grasps at nothing. Criticism can only take up its role when based on reliable facts. Often, we cannot even define the problem situation, as there is too much uncertainty about the state of our theories; we do not know where they break down, since the facts themselves are far from unambiguous.

The common sense view of scientific progress is thus a precondition to Popper's view of scientific progress. We first need to focus on reliable facts, only then we can move to critical discussions of our theories. We need to make our empirical studies reliable before we can move on and use them as criticism of our theories, otherwise we may produce false feedback that stops us from overthrowing false theories with true theories and even causes us to replace true theories with false theories.

In fact, in economics, theory and empirics have decoupled more and more from each other since the late 1990s; there is much fewer direct connection between theory and much of empirics today than there was some decades ago (Biddle and Hamermesh 2017). If both theory and empirics tend to meander more independently from each other, scientific progress will become more erratic. In case studies are not tightly connected to a theoretical setup, they tend to pile up on each other, with ad-hoc comparison to past results.

A literature consisting only of empirical studies can drift around rather aimlessly. Without thinking through the mechanisms that lead to the creation of our facts, facts by themselves are not very meaningful; to make sense, facts need to be integrated together with other facts. A mere accumulation of estimates will merely lead us into false feedback bubbles.

A false feedback bubble emerges when studies in a field produce false feedback and other studies take up this false feedback to produce their own false feedback, on top of it, such that the direction of research in the entire field deviates from empirical reality in unpredictable ways.

To illustrate, imagine a bad singer, without much introspection, who is always told by her too kind friends that she is a great singer. She may intensify her hobby more and more and even think about a career as a professional singer. Due to lack of connection to reality, she lives on in her very own false feedback bubble. The life of Florence Foster Jenkins provides an almost too perfect example for this. Jenkins was widely known as the world's worst opera singer. Despite her complete lack of talent, her friends always supported her, and no one told Jenkins in her privately organized recitals that, in reality, she could not sing at all and constantly missed the right notes.

True and false feedback are distinct from positive and negative feedback. Positive feedback is information that increases deviation from the original state. Negative feedback is information that decreases deviation from the original state by reverting to it. An equilibrium is an extreme case of negative feedback, a so-called limiting case. True feedback generally causes negative feedback; it brings the researcher closer to the true state of things. In contrast, false feedback can cause positive or negative feedback, and its relation to truth, the original state, becomes arbitrary.

Existing empirical research serves as a natural basis for the conduct of future empirical research. However, if researchers build on previous empirical research that is false, it can happen that the entire field loses track and moves ever further away from the true state of things. The decisive element here will always be how strong the illusion of true feedback is. Because independent knowledge of the structures of reality is impossible, assessment of whether the finding of a previous study is real can be difficult. Researchers can thus slide into larger or smaller false feedback bubbles, which means that they create elaborate structures with only little foundation in reality.

For example, take the seemingly very true study of Reinhart and Rogoff (2010). This study finds that countries with more than 90% government debt show lower median GDP growth rates. A lot of subsequent research incorporated this result of a 90% threshold, and it even entered the political debate on financial austerity. However, as chance would have it, an undergraduate student proved this result of a 90% threshold wrong. After an intense battle, he even managed to publish his replication study in an academic journal (Herndon et al. 2014). The study of Herndon et al. (2014) shows that the main results of Reinhart and Rogoff (2010) were caused by "selective exclusion of available data, coding errors, and inappropriate weighting of summary statistics". The study of Reinhardt and Rogoff (2010) is therefore an illustrative example for a study that kicked loose a false feedback bubble. If it were not for the effort of the undergraduate student, we would probably never have known about the falsity of this very popular result of a 90% debt threshold. Such incidents of illusions of true feedback raise the question in what kind of other false feedback bubbles we may be living right now.

Nissen et al. (2016) model how false feedback can become canonized, meaning that researchers widely accept it as true. They describe this canonization against the background that facts are accepted as true because the research community accepts them as true, not because they adequately represent reality. This makes it possible that false facts can enter the basic understanding of researchers. Most research seldom independently tests the exact same hypothesis but rather constructs of hypotheses, which, if they refer to some common, underlying hypothesis, lend support it. Thus, most research consists not of direct replications but of distinct studies referring to and thus indirectly supporting the same broad hypothesis. Together they yield evidence for a particular hypothesis and canonize it as a false fact. Nissen et al. (2016) present publication bias as the driver behind the canonization of false facts. If only positive results are published, the research community observes only those studies falsely supporting the false facts. Combating this problem would require the publication of negative results, too, otherwise the false feedback goes unchallenged. However, in the presence of p-hacking, even the publication of negative results will not be sufficient to stop the canonization of false feedback, as p-hacking disturbs the evidential basis of our conclusions regarding the false facts.

Many researchers uphold that over time the literature as a whole will in any case uncover clear tendencies that identify true feedback and eliminate false feedback. Together, the studies in a field create a wall of evidence in favor or against a certain hypothesis. Otherwise, it would be impossible that numerous separate studies come to similar conclusions. However, there is increasing evidence that even a large number of studies in a given field can lend support to insights that constitute false feedback (Zwaan et al. 2018). Researcher degrees of freedom, statistical noise, and publication bias can together "assemble a seemingly solid set of studies that appear to support an underlying theory, even though no single study from that set could survive a direct replication attempt" (Zwaan et al. 2018). Zwaan et al. (2018) argue that there are, by now, many examples of theories and effects that have been supported by "dozens, if not hundreds" of studies that have collapsed in systematic replication attempts. Researcher degrees of freedom, statistical noise, and publication bias can be tools so powerful that they create evidence in the form of a "wall full of defective bricks" (Zwaan et al. 2018).

One difference between practical tasks and economics is that the practical tasks create the world, whereas economics tries to read the world they create. We are mere observers and do not create the world ourselves. In biological evolution, for example, organisms adapt because of their competitiveness with respect to their environment. The laws of nature set limits, too, but biological evolution contains a large creative element. There is no fixed path where biological evolution will converge toward. In science, in contrast, given true feedback, theories tend to converge to the truth over time; they are only free in their paths when there is also false feedback. In an ideal world of true feedback, economics would map what exists out there in reality. Theories would not themselves be free to meaner around, but they roughly follow how economic reality actually looks like. True feedback constrains theories to stick to how things are. In sharp contrast, false feedback can lead theories very astray, far away from reality. False feedback bubbles contain a large creative element.

The feedback process thus determines whether we discover reality or create reality. The classic view of science, as learning from nature, is a limiting case in the presence of true feedback. In case of false feedback, scientists can pursue to construct their own worlds. This creation of the world due to false feedback is accidental, that is, without any intention on behalf of the researchers. They just do not know any better, as they have no independent access to reality. The overall results are very creative worldviews, which are themselves less connected to reality. The false feedback generated in the social sciences gives rise to an enormous diversity of different ideas, which also make the social sciences colorful, sometimes turning them into a technically highly advanced form of art.

False feedback bubbles closely relate to the concept of "fooled by randomness" (Taleb 2001). The latter describes instances where a person attributes a series of chance outcomes to his personal skills. If, for example, the actions of a trader active in financial markets are mostly determined by chance, the trader may not realize this, and nevertheless perceive these chance outcomes as the result of his own skills. If the trader experiences success in his past trades, he will feel high-skilled; if he experiences failure, he will feel low-skilled (or simply stupid), even though most of it was just chance. Similarly, a researcher observes whether the hypothesis he formulated turns out as either true or false; he will save up both these outcomes in his memory and thus perceive them as constantly increasing his knowledge. However, if the feedback the researcher receives is mostly false, this process creates a steadily growing illusion of knowledge. While false feedback may provide reasons for either corroboration or falsification of a given theory, the researcher feels more and more confident about his subject. The disguise of randomness as skill in the case of the trader in financial market is thus equivalent to the disguise of false feedback as knowledge in the case of the researcher. The researcher is certain that his knowledge has increased, while in reality he is just moving within a false feedback bubble.

Science only makes progress if the trial and error results in visible errors. The incentive needs to be there to find errors and expose them. However, nobody has incentives to actually detect errors (i.e., false feedback), because they seldom publish well and are thus not relevant for anyone. Even though they are probably even more important than novelties, they largely hide from us.

Thus, a large problem in economics is the difficulty to eliminate false theories. Every theory, which has ever been thought of, is still somewhere around and, from time to time, even reappears on stage again (see, e.g., Frey and Iselin 2017). In the natural sciences, falsified theories vanish and, outside history of science classes, will never reappear back on stage. In economics, in contrast, we can always argue against theories we think are false, but it is hardly possible to fully disprove them. This difficulty of conclusive falsification is one of the culprits for the disorder in the economic literature.

Because the high variation in empirical feedback makes it very difficult to rely on previous results, theorists have an especially hard time knowing on which findings among the myriad of contradicting findings they can rely on. Theorists thus let other factors decide the basis of their theories, real-world observations or impressive descriptive statistics, for instance, where there is much fewer variation, as these types of facts are much more stable and less subject to the danger of reverting again over the next few years. Theorists can hardly be blamed for this. No theorist wants to build a model if he or she runs the risk of erecting this model on false feedback. Important historical occurrences, such as the Great Recession, are therefore much more valuable input for theorists.

In the absence of powerful empirical tests, scientists will not give up their theories and adopt new theories, since one has no way of knowing whether they describe reality better. Akerlof and Michaillat (2018) argue that even moderate levels of homophily, which is the tendency to grant tenure to young scientists with similar views, can block the transition to new theories. They therefore infer that, since economics lacks powerful empirical tests, especially macroeconomics, it will continue to have substantial trouble moving toward better theories.

Even worse, empirical economists sometimes rely on strong theoretical priors and produce false feedback in line with them. For instance, Card and Krueger (1995) show that studies on minimum wages censor non-negative employment effects. Researchers (unconsciously) p-hack their obtained results until they find "evidence" corroborating their theoretical priors. Doucouliagos and Stanely (2013) go as far as to argue that theory determines the distribution of empirical results. Fields monopolized by one dominant theory show less variation in empirical results than fields where theory is more contested. Because studies that are at odds with the dominant theory may be incredible in the eyes of the community, researchers tend to alter their results until they are close enough to the prediction of the dominant theory. In contested fields, in contrast, researchers can publish a wider array of results, as they are more theoretically acceptable, and the field will show greater variation.

Thus, in the presence of p-hacking, a dominant theory may turn into a disadvantage, as it forces empirical research into line. In case of only true feedback, a dominant theory is clearly superior, as it carves out exactly where empirical research can attack it. Corroboration and falsification of the dominant theory can then point toward its strength and weaknesses and pave the way for its improvement, or even make way for the creation of entirely new theories. However, as long as p-hacking is widespread, a dominant theory cannot unfold its potential. It may constrain the emergence of certain false feedback bubbles, but this comes at the cost of creating illusory evidence for the theory itself. Once again, to reap the full potential of a dominant theory, reliable facts and therefore true feedback are needed. They will furthermore deliver the required facts upon which new theories can be erected.

9 The tree of knowledge

As an undergraduate, I used to think of economics as a magnificent tree of knowledge with a strong and stable foundation and a wide emerging top divided into numerous finer branches. I thought the trunk of this tree of knowledge to consist of the most fundamental findings all economists agree on, whereas the top would encompass the more tentative findings where there is still disagreement. I also imagined all these numerous findings to be somehow connected to each other. If there were exclusively true feedback, the sum of all economic studies may indeed give rise to such large-scale mutual complementarity. However, in the presence of false feedback, it becomes impossible to objectively merge different economic studies into a coherent and organized whole, as the illusion of true feedback makes it very difficult to know on which studies to rely on. The only way to organize studies in a field abound with false feedback is to (heavily) distort their contents. Nonetheless, to be able to publish, we have each time to present the entire empirical literature as such an internally consistent tree of knowledge. Every researcher is required to force the entirety of the disordered literature into a unified discussion resembling a coherent whole again, and in this has to bend the empirical results of most studies.

If one reads the literature review of only a single study, the entire literature on the topic seems to be neatly in line. The world starts to look already quite different after having read the literature review of a second and third study. The deeper one goes in reading all of the relevant studies in the literature, the more the actual disorder of the literature starts to surface, only for that every researcher in the end has to force everything into line again for his or her own literature review. In order to guarantee the internal consistency of their own studies, researchers have to sacrifice the actual state of the empirical literature and mold it according to the respective needs of their own studies. Otherwise, their own studies cannot uphold the impression of making a clear contribution to the literature. Thus, if researchers want to present their own ideas in good light, they need to cut through various caveats, which would otherwise pose a problem to their storyline. This use of force is only possible because no researcher has a very detailed oversight over all the relevant aspects present in the manifold of previous empirical studies. If some time has elapsed after reading a given study, one can only remember its central insights. This makes it easy for researchers to violate more nuanced aspects of previous studies.

In the presence of false feedback, writing a literature review is akin to squaring the circle. If researchers try to take into account certain answers given by the existing literature, this will open up their argument to criticism given by other answers in the existing literature. It is similar to attempts at creating a two-dimensional map of the earth. When researchers try to map the literature so that they can get the east-west aspect right, they distort the north-south aspect. If they change the literature to get the north-south aspect right, they distort the east-west aspect. It is impossible to give adequate credit to all existing literature, as this would inhibit a proper storyline for one's own study.

To circumvent the problem of a literature abound with false feedback, researchers often resort to cherry-picking studies that allow for good comparisons. This is yet another manifestation of confirmation bias. Researchers incorporate only those studies that align nicely with their own studies. They cite studies that fit their storyline and allow for carving out of a more promising research niche.

Truth in literature reviews is thus often a matter of making. This explains why "framing" of the study is the most important aspect for successful publication. The literature has to be arranged in a way that opens up a spot that seems truly novel to others, even though this spot may be artificial.

Instead of a tedious ordering of the previous empirical literature, researchers can also resort to simpler alternatives that evade substantial complications with existing studies, because they do not impose high demands on the mutual consistency with past empirical studies. For example, in the form of "previous literature has shown that A, B, and C have an effect on Y. We contribute to this growing literature by showing an effect of D on Y". This approach avoids the problem of in-depth comparisons with previous empirical studies, since the effects are presumed to be additive. In a typical setting, all studies A, B, C, and of course also D, will claim to have found large causal effects on Y. Only few researchers see a contradiction in the fact that we regularly observe numerous studies arguing to have found the one crucial determinant of a certain variable. However, this runs into what Gelman (2017) calls the "piranha problem". Too many large effects eat each other up. Because variation of the dependent variable Y is limited, the existence of many independent large effects is impossible. By choosing to portray their contributions to the literature as the additional causal estimate D, the researchers avoid facing the problem that there is actually no more room left for D. If they had analyzed the connections between A, B, C, and D, they would have realized that at least some of them would need to be false. An even less controversial approach is to simply state that "this paper relates/contributes to literatures X, Y, and Z", without even laying out the exact differences. This completely avoids any confrontation with the fact that the relevant literature consists of incompatible findings.

Contributing one further isolated causal estimate to the literature also avoids stepping on someone else's feet. One does not have to discuss to what extent the study conflicts with other important studies in the literature, and all researchers can continue undisturbed to push through their own findings. Although this attitude is detrimental to knowledge, it is a very rational response, because other researchers meet attempts at falsification of their own studies with fierce resistance. The career of every economist rises and falls with the popularity of his or her own studies. Even though the authors of the original study would probably be best suited to judge whether a particular critique of their study is relevant or not, they will naturally dismiss it, because a falsification of their own study will damage their citation count. Whether the self-interest coupled to the popularity of an empirical economic study is beneficial to the progress of knowledge is therefore debatable. The personal benefits researchers obtain from a specific popular idea can rapidly collapse into the Sophist attitude of deliberately turning the weaker argument into the stronger, even if they themselves know that their studies are rather far from true feedback. Of course, other researchers are perfectly free in their judgment of which studies best approach true feedback. However, the illusion of true feedback makes initial decisions about the quality of newly published studies difficult, and if a researcher has once hopped on the bus, he or she has stakes in it, too, and will consequently fight for the respective idea as well.

When studies introduce new elements to the literature, they often do so without explicitly analyzing how these new elements differentiate them from previous studies. Referring to some potential reasons why we should observe certain differences between two studies is usually sufficient to demarcate them from each other. However, most statements claiming that "our results X differ from results Y because" are mere suggestions without the provision of any substantiating evidence. Actually, it would be most interesting to empirically test whether these are indeed the reasons why two studies deliver different results, through, for instance, alternative model specifications that reduce to an explicit mutual comparison between them. Although not always feasible, this would allow us to obtain an empirical estimate of the influence of at least some of our most important forking paths.

The whole idea of finding and occupying a research niche is not very useful in its current form in empirical economics. Skilled researchers will always be able to open up by force a well-defined research niche in the existing literature. However, this research niche will be an artificial spot within a false unity. An intense discussion of just the two or three most closely related studies of each study would provide a much more valuable contribution to the literature. The researchers would have to directly compare the aspects of their study with the aspects of these other studies and work out on what dimension they are the same and how they differ from each other. Such direct comparison to only a few studies would allow for verification of the ways taken through the garden of forking paths, by, for example, showing which researcher degrees of freedom are very decisive and exert a large effect on the obtained empirical results. Important is that the selected studies are not cherry-picked to allow for favorable comparisons. Ideally, the selected studies would show contradictory findings, which could then be disentangled with the help of the study at hand. Thus, instead of discussing a large number of studies very superficially, intense discussion of only a few studies could open up a critical debate about their most important aspects and thus cause actual progress in the literature.

10 The locality of knowledge

The importance of framing a study is also the result of the highly fragmented knowledge in today's economics. Each study needs to be tailored to the existing knowledge of its respective audience. Depending on which journal they want to submit, researchers often need to rewrite the entire storyline of their study. Most economists are so heavily specialized that they have no idea what is going on in other fields; most knowledge is thus only locally present. To still be able to communicate with other heavily specialized economists, researchers need to adapt the framing of their study accordingly.

This increasing specialization is visible in the raising average team size in scientific research. Wuchty et al. (2007) document an increasing dominance of team work across nearly all scientific fields. In the social sciences more specifically, the average team size has increased from somewhat more than one to more than two over the period 1960–2000. The division of labor has thus reached scientific work as well. This brings, on the one hand, the productivity advantage of specialization, while, on the other hand, it erects further barriers for mutual understanding among researchers. Moreover, knowledge concentrated in a single mind tends to be more consistent than knowledge spread over many minds.

Knowledge has also become narrower in the topics empirical work investigates. Researchers have increasingly started to zoom in into the analysis of certain (economic) events. Instead of pursuing broadly applicable correlational studies, which too often suffer from unresolvable issues of endogeneity, researchers focus on specific circumstances that allow the identification of causal effects. This movement is what Angrist and Pischke (2010) have termed the "credibility revolution". Researchers, just like detectives, are watching out for all sorts of exogenous shocks or natural experiments. In practice, this has led to the phenomenon that the interest is mainly on the identification strategy, while the actual economic relevance of the study is somewhat secondary. The estimated effect has to be causal, and the more causal, the better. This development has further strengthened the emphasis in empirical economics on what is feasible and less on what is economically relevant. In fact, the strong focus on randomization to identify economic effects has led to an almost equally strong randomization of contributions across research topics, all varying widely in content and with many of them only remotely connected to economics (see, e.g., Freakonomics by Levitt and Dubner (2005)). The question is of course whether such local estimates of causality also translate into more broadly applicable insights.

A general, albeit unfortunate, rule is that the better causality is identified, the less relevant it becomes. In most applied studies, there exists a trade-off between internal and external validity. Studies with a high internal validity tend to have a low external validity, while studies with high external validity tend to have a low internal validity. Experiments are more typical of the former type of studies, while observational studies are more typical of the latter type.

Nonetheless, in studies exploiting causal links internal validity is too often taken to imply external validity. Causal effects do not take place in a vacuum though. They depend on the context within which they happen. If one or several factors contributing to their emergence are different, the causal effects may not be present anymore. Factors supporting the causal effect could be absent, while others could absorb it. They may be small and numerous, or large and few, such as functioning institutions. Too often we simply assume that the causal results would hold up in other contexts as well.

For instance, a descriptive statistic from a given context is seldom regarded as representative for other contexts, because each statistic reflects the influence of a myriad of factors. In contrast, a causal effect is regarded much more readily as representative for other contexts, even though for the causal effect to take place, it, too, depends on the influence of a myriad of factors. A descriptive statistic does not depend on less factors contributing to its emergence than a causal effect.

In economics specific policies are often taken as representative for a certain category of policies, even though important idiosyncratic properties can make them very different from other policies belonging to this same category. Wells and Windschitl (1999) show how experimental treatments taken from a category with high internal variance can lead to strongly biased estimates. In psychology, for example, specific people often constitute the treatment and control group for categories such as race, age, or gender. For instance, to differentiate between how people react differently to men and women, researchers run an experiment where they expose a large sample of participants to either a male or a female actor. In such a scenario, even if the sample is perfectly randomized between treatment and control, the gender treatment is not. Both the male and female actor can exhibit important idiosyncratic characteristics, such that the treatment is not representative for the category "gender". Stimulus sampling can correct for this problem; the researchers would need to study several treatment and control cases with different male and female actors. The same problem applies to most treatment effects in economics. The unique properties of specific policies can lead to widely varying treatment effects, which are not themselves representative of the category of policies they should be.

The representativeness of treatments is not the only concern for the generalizability of experimental results. Yarkoni (2019) points out that claims about a hypothesis are only valid if theoretical and statistical expressions closely align with each other. Otherwise, researchers will commit an unjustified generalization of their results. Yarkoni (2019) argues that, for instance, in psychology many studies make verbal claims that are only little connected to the statistical quantities they rely on. Further elements that determine the generalizability of experimental results are sample of subjects, experimental task, instructions, experimenters, research sites, testing room, culture, or even minor aspects such as time of day, weather, lighting conditions, etc. (Yarkoni 2019). They all create variability that vastly increases the uncertainty around the main experimental estimate. Nonetheless, researchers often interpret the particular operationalization they chose for their experiment as a representative test of their much broader, verbal hypothesis. They assume that all other potential sources for variation like the experimental tasks are exactly zero. In contrast, Yarkoni (2019) shows that even moderate variation in these combined sources can hugely increase the uncertainty intervals of the main estimate.

Moreover, no economic environment stays the same over time. A study may indeed have been able to single out true feedback, but when in all other studies the environment is different, there is not much substance attached to the identified causality after all. It was something that emerged only in a very specific environment, at a specific time and place. Just as the Greek philosopher Heraclitus (around 530–460 BC) had it: "No man can ever step in the same river twice, for it is not the same river". Each time you step into the river, the stream of running water will be different. Even studies that manage to show true feedback may in fact produce only spatially and temporally applicable results.

Economists have been very creative for the last three decades in exploiting various events at different times and places in order to get at causal estimates. They have become experts in locating various identification strategies in every comprehensive dataset they lay hands on. A single dataset can give rise to numerous opportunities to identify causal effects. Yet the applicability of these causal effects is then restricted to the respective time and place as well. To be able to generalize the causality, the researcher would need to carry out the same identification strategy at different times and places, too. For example, a perfectly identified wage elasticity of a certain region in a country will not necessarily be helpful if we want to know the wage elasticities of other regions in the country. For this, we would need a lot of additional knowledge about how the different regions relate to each other. Causal effects estimated at different times and places only converge if all of the respective local environments are adequately controlled for. Otherwise, the local circumstances imply that the estimated causal effects are local, too. We will never obtain a wage elasticity that is exactly the same in every region.

In the presence of always true feedback, this would not pose a major problem. To the contrary, the variety in local estimates could provide us with rich information about the specific conditions of economic reality. It would be the equivalent of trial and error resulting in repeated true feedback. The abundance of information would allow us to reliably falsify and improve our economic theories. In the presence of false feedback, however, local estimates are detrimental, because studies originating from different environments do not allow for comparisons to eliminate variation in empirical feedback.

Gelman (2013) describes the representativeness of a causal effect in three scenarios. First, essentially no effect: the variation in the effects of the individual studies comes from variation in the garden of forking paths, the respective effects are just false positives. Second, large and variable effects: the size of the effects depends on the respective environment the studies take place in. Third, large and consistent effects: the effects of the individual studies are all of a similar size, irrespective of the environment. In the first case, we live in a false feedback bubble, wherever it may move us. In the second case, we need to be able to separate out the influence of the different environments. Only in the last case the causal effects estimated in individual studies would be representative of each other.

The problem that changing economic environments can inhibit identifying effects is far-reaching. It could exceed the problem of the garden of forking paths by far: the variation within the garden of forking paths may be smaller than the variation between the different economic environments. However, before we can make any assessments about how much variation in economic environments affects our estimates, we need to have reliable estimates about the impact of the garden of forking paths. Otherwise, we run into an identification problem. Because we have two sources of unobserved variation, economic environments and the garden of forking paths, we have no idea why a study worked here and not there. We first need to fix the core of our studies, to find a way to better approach true feedback in every single study, only then we can move on. The last chapter of the book will take up this issue. For now, let us assume that we were able to identify local estimates in a reliable way.

In this, knowledge of locally identified causal effects can be very helpful for policy makers in the respective regions, because it provides information about their immediate environments. Even from the perspective of the entire country, well-identified local estimates can be more useful for policy makers than less well-identified, more global estimates. Policy makers may only have information about one particular region, this particular information will be much more solid though.

The idea is to restrict the consequences of a policy to the local (Taleb 2012). Policy makers at the local level have to decide whether they are willing to introduce a policy with potentially far-reaching consequences ("policy makers" can refer to all kinds of actors in a democracy). If just one or a few locations do so, and the policy does not work out, the negative consequences will be restricted to just the local environment, too. In contrast, if the policy does work out, and repeatedly so in different local settings, the policy might be safe to introduce to most other local environments as well.

Hayek (1973) describes our complex modern societies as reliant on customs, habits, or practices, which are not the product of deliberate human design, but have developed through the combined and mutually adjusted trial and error of generations of people. Some of these rules may not seem rational, because they make no sense in light of our current scientific theories. However, the fact that they have survived until today implies that they must be of at least some importance, even though this may not be obvious on the surface. Many people cannot accept such hidden knowledge; they contest to have a holistic understanding of the entire economy and thus intend to improve it accordingly. However, large political interventions also lead to large unforeseen consequences. We always like to emphasize the positive consequences of each political change, while we remain silent about all the possible negative consequences, often because we cannot possibly know them in advance. The introduction of a new law may indeed lead to the intended positive economic effects, but it will also cause at least some unintended, often adverse economic effects. Hayek (1973) argues that the degree of control we can exercise over a spontaneous order like an economy is much smaller than the degree of control we could exercise over a made order, like an individual firm. Many aspects of a spontaneous order cannot be controlled by us at all, or at least not without severe interference with the entire spontaneous order. A spontaneous order arises because each individual balances its own actions against all the respective circumstances to which it is exposed. This balance will be destroyed through the interventions of someone without precise knowledge of these individual circumstances.

Evolutionary systems are often perceived as something very stable one can do no harm to. Yet this is a gross misunderstanding; they often function under rather delicate balances, which may individually seem unnecessary at first. It can be very difficult for researchers to recognize the most important relationships at play in an evolutionary system, be it in nature or in the economy, since most of them make sense only when the system is adequately traced in its entirety, including all relationships.

This does not imply that simple "laissez-faire" is always superior though. I think we are obliged to trying to better our economic situations actively, especially if there appear substantial problems. In line with Popper (1945, 1957), I argue that our political interventions should be piecemeal, meaning that they should be step-wise and cautious, and that we should always watch out for potentially unforeseen errors caused by the way the entire system adapts. We should thereby try to constantly learn from the errors of our piecemeal political actions and correct them along the way accordingly.

This includes piecemeal policies with potentially far-reaching consequences, which must follow the same cautious trial and error process. No policy maker will be able to predict all of the consequences of a newly introduced policy. Policies with a large impact are very likely to lead to conflict with the economy. Every major policy, introduced with the objective to improve the economy, is likely to cause problems somewhere else in the economy. Hence, as outlined, a possible solution to this problem is a restriction to the local (Taleb 2012). A major policy should only be applied more broadly if repeated trials on different local levels have indicated that the policy is safe. In this, empirical evidence shedding light on particular local environments can be very valuable, as it provides policy makers with more exact information about what to expect if they indeed implemented major new policies.

The present situation in empirical economics with its many well-identified, small-scale causal studies, which typically exhibit rather low external validity, may thus have its positive side, since they can provide us with reliable information about whether a particular piecemeal policy intervention may be helpful or not. In contrast, less well-identified, large-scale empirical studies depict reality less accurately, and can, because of their potentially large unintended consequences, not be safely applied to policy interventions. Hence, while the search for causal identification does indeed reduce the relevance of the research questions to some extent, we get lucky sometimes. If a well-identified causal effect coincides with an upcoming question of high political relevance, it can guide the implementation of a well-designed piecemeal policy; first locally, and then, if broadly successful, more globally.

11 Machine learning and sample splits

The success of machine learning has naturally opened up the question whether its tools may be useful for economists, too. However, there is a fundamental difference between empirical economics and machine learning: while economists try to understand phenomena, machine learning is mostly concerned with prediction. Machine learning tries to predict outcomes with maximal accuracy, making overfitting the most relevant concern. The target is to infer from the data the statistical model that can predict best; the statistical model needs to be maximally generalizable to similar situations. How exactly the detected statistical model predicts or looks like is less important. The point is whether it can correctly assign all of its inputs to the respective outputs. Economists, on the other hand, want to identify the underlying causes.

Machine learning has thrived so much over the last decade because it has applied its statistical tools mostly to practical tasks. In every application, the performance of a machine learning model can only be as good as the data it relies on allow it. If we feed the algorithm input data that are not able to adequately map the output data, the machine learning model extracted by the algorithm will fail in its application, as the information about the environment will be false; the machine learning model learns based on false feedback. Hence, machine learning methods are best suited for tasks where the question about what constitutes relevant input data able to map the output data is unambiguous. In the case of a machine learning model applied to self-driving cars, for instance, there are no questions about the direct and real connection between the car's sensors or cameras and the steering of the car. If the algorithm is fed a sufficient amount of data from the right sensors or cameras, it has all the information necessary for correct prediction; there are, for instance, no issues of omitted variables. The algorithm can detect a functional relationship able to correctly map all the input data to the output. If the data cover all of the relevant environment, the prediction errors will correspond to true feedback, and the algorithm can rely on true information about why it did work out or not and improve accordingly.

The performance of a machine learning model thus depends on how well one selects both input data and output data. If there indeed exists a true model, a well-applied machine learning algorithm will detect it. Uninformative input data does thereby not cause large problems, as it will get small weights. Important is only to have a sufficient amount of relevant input data.

The most widely cited example of the power of machine learning methods such as deep learning is probably their ability to correctly assign images to different categories, such as whether an image contains a certain object or not. In order to do so, a deep learning algorithm is fed with millions of real-life images that either depict situations with the object in it or situations without it. If the images capture a broad enough spectrum of relevant situations, the algorithm has everything it requires to generate correct predictions; no other variables are lacking in such a case. The central ingredient to train the deep learning algorithm is that human operators beforehand designate every image that contains the object. The algorithm then uses this information in its repeated trials to correctly predict whether an image indeed contains the object. It does so through shooting back and forth between making predictions and adjusting the parameters to its prediction errors. After many series of such updates, the algorithm will have generated a deep learning model that is able to assign the individual images via a complex function to the correct categories. Thus, machine learning methods like deep learning are so successful in these kinds of practical tasks because they can rely on unambiguous answers to whether they have predicted correctly or not. They constantly receive true feedback about their own performance. False feedback only occurs if either the images do not capture well the possible spectrum of relevant situations or if the human operators have assigned images to the wrong categories. The adjustments of the parameters will become finer and finer over the repeated trials, until the deep learning model can differentiate between minute details. In practical tasks, the algorithm always "knows" where it stands and whether and by how much it needs to change to improve its own predictions.

Alternatively, take the example of e-mail requests by a firm's customers. Based on analysis of answers to previous e-mail requests, a statistical model can propose a tentative answer, together with a corresponding level of confidence. A human operator can then approve the answer, providing the machine learning algorithm with true feedback that it has predicted correctly, which subsequently increases its confidence in generating answers. Otherwise, if the human operator does not approve of the answer, he or she provides the algorithm with true feedback that it has predicted wrongly. Instead, the human operator feeds the machine learning algorithm with a new, tailor-made answer to the e-mail request. The algorithm will use this additional piece of information in order to update its own parameters and thus improve the statistical model and with it also the generation of new answers. Over time, the more information about adequate matches between both e-mail requests and answers the algorithm can rely on, the better the answers to all the possible requests will become.

A trained machine learning model is highly context dependent. If the relevant environment experiences substantial changes, the model will become lost, as it will fail to generalize to the altered conditions. A machine learning model can only predict within the very same environment it was trained in. If the rules of the games change, it has no possibility to adapt. The only way to set the model up again is to train it with data from the changed environment. This is contrary to the aims of empirical economics; by identifying causality, economists intend to predict ex-ante what will happen in case the environment experiences substantial changes. Needless to say that economics faces a more difficult task than machine learning. Prediction within what we already know is a much simpler challenge.

If a self-driving car has an accident, the engineers have to go back and improve the machine learning model accordingly. This corresponds to the ultimate embodiment of true feedback. In empirical economics, this type of feedback is quite rare, and if it happens, researchers are quick to introduce some excuse and then still go on to use the very same model again. This happens mainly because, while a badly searched machine learning model lets cars to crash, a badly searched econometric result, even if it later turns out to be false, has usually only very few practical consequences.

Machine learning tackles its central problem of overfitting the data by the use of sample splits. The question in applied machine learning is always whether the detected model generalizes to sets of new data points, too. This is typically done by dividing the data randomly into a training set, a cross-validation set, and a test set. The training set serves to estimate various differently specified models. These models naturally fit the training set very well and will thus return relatively low model error. If the applied model has sufficient flexibility, it can explain almost every detail of the training set. This is problematic, since in this case it does not only capture relevant information but also a lot of statistical noise. The latter inhibits successful prediction in different environments, where the statistical noise will inevitably be different. The choice for the best model has thus to be made on the basis of so far unused data. This is what the cross-validation set is used for. The best model is usually the one which shows the lowest model error in the cross-validation set. To report the model error of the final specification, the test set is applied. The cross-validation set will underestimate the actual model error, to, as it served for the choice of the best model, which is again a manifestation of the overfitting problem.

This approach of using sample splits to combat overfitting may actually provide a promising way to combat the adverse effects of p-hacking. For example, researchers could try out as many model specifications on the training set as they wish. However, they would need to show whether their preferred specifications perform well on the cross-validation set as well. If the statistical significance of these specifications evaporates, they are likely to have been the result of statistical noise. In contrast, if the preferred specifications uphold in the cross-validation set, too, they are likely to generalize to at least the data at hand. Importantly, the final specifications as published in the study would have to be run on the test set. This corrects for the fact that the final specifications have been chosen because of their performance on the cross-validation set. This constant double-checking for potential overfitting makes the generation of false positives unlikely. It would still be possible to actively p-hack over all three subsamples. However, the use of sample splits would make such p-hacking extremely time consuming, because the specifications would have to fit all three subsamples. In practice, researchers would have to present their results for all of their three subsamples. Only robust specifications representing actual patterns of the data will survive such an application of a threefold sample split.

The caveat of the sample split approach is of course that it needs more data. For example, standard country-year panel datasets will not provide a sufficient number of observations to allow a random allocation into separate subsamples. The approach will thus be more appropriate in cases of, for instance, data generated through digital interactions. Moreover, the estimated p-values will be much more conservative. If a researcher splits his or her sample into three subsamples, the drop in observations will increase the standard errors. Because the standard error is divided by the square root of the sample size, this increase is not three times as large; the standard errors of the subsamples will be an expected 73% larger than the standard errors of the full sample. However, this corresponds to a one time and generalized adjustment of all standard errors that is much smaller than, for example, multiple comparisons corrections for repeated trials would demand it.

A problem of the sample split approach is the lack of credible commitment. Researchers could split their samples ex-post, after they have searched their results over the full sample. This runs contrary to the very purpose of the exercise. To solve this problem, Fafchamps and Labonne (2017) argue that a third party could step in as supervisor in the sample splitting process. For instance, the AEA could create a website where external data providers can upload their datasets, and a team of independent employees at the AEA then randomly splits the data into subsamples, with scrambled IDs, and sends only the training set to researchers, while keeping the rest of the data as the hold out test set. This would be feasible for data collected through intermediaries or for proprietary data originating from firms or public administrations. Sample split approaches will be less credible in cases where the whole dataset is already publicly available, as the researchers could access these available datasets and undo the separation into subsamples. Fafchamps and Labonne (2017) argue that sample split approaches are especially valuable if there is large room for exploratory data analysis. Researchers can test many alternative hypotheses and their possible refinements on the training set they receive, and only after acceptance of the study they would run their by this way pre-specified analysis on the test set.

Importantly, the use of sample splits allows to subject p-hacked patterns in the data to falsification. If researchers p-hack and do not adjust their p-values accordingly, the results they will unearth are not yet empirically tested. They were subject to way too high p-value thresholds and did thus not confront any possibility of rejection. In contrast, if the p-hacked statistical specifications are run on the test set as final step, they will have withstood an attempt at falsification. Of course, because sample splits are samples drawn from the same population, they constitute a comparatively weaker attempt at falsification. Samples drawn from different populations would entail more demanding empirical tests, as they indicate higher levels of generality. Nevertheless, the use of a test set for the final step can at least fix the problem surrounding invalid p-values. The random assignment of the data into different subsamples breaks with the statistical noise patterns. The test set contains alternative patterns of noise and thus makes statistical tests that separate relevant information from noise valid again.

12 Practical experience

A lot of today's economic research is conducted away from daily economic life. Yet sound economic research operates in continuous exchange with important economic events. Daily economic life generates problems research should offer corresponding solutions to. Otherwise economics starts to drift into art. Economists are not demanded in this world because they perform some skillful art, but because they are able to provide adequate solutions to important economic problems. If the general public would indeed start to perceive economists as artists, funding would collapse rather quickly.

One way to bring us closer to (useful) true feedback in economics could be practical work experience. It could help researchers to come up with new economic theories, and, importantly, strengthen their ability to sort out very unrealistic theories. This is of special importance for studies in management and finance. Before being able to write sensibly about these topics, one would need at least some experience as entrepreneur, manager, or trader. For instance, Taleb (2018) argues that one can only understand management and finance by doing it and not by reading about it. In economics, in contrast, obtaining practical work experience is more difficult. Economics goes well beyond what can be perceived by the individual; its aim is to get an adequate overview over all relevant elements of the economy. Nevertheless, a position at a central bank, a large firm, or the government may still sharpen understanding of how decision makers act in light of their respective environment. After some years of practical work experience, researchers could then step back and try to develop theories to explain what they have observed. If they are indeed able to propose a promising new theory, they could go on to test it with an adequate empirical strategy. As every other theory, it will need to satisfy intersubjective objectivity; its predictions need to hold up in different contexts. Practical work experience does clearly not have the potential to replace the methods of economic research, but it could enrich it with crucial new stimuli and hold back the creation of false theories.

Practical experience could serve as a benchmark against which theories can be evaluated. By comparing the theories with practical experience, anomalies will start to turn up, areas where the theory breaks down. Such anomalies cannot only falsify the theory but they can also be the ingredients to the development of new entirely new theories.

Even Plato (trans. 1888), the father of all rationalists, intended to put all future philosopher kings "down the den again" through extensive practical experience in the daily economic activity of the common people. At the age of 35, after years of studying, including 5 years of dialectic, the highest of the arts, potential candidates would have had to master 15 years of "experience of life", to test whether they understood philosophy and stand firm to the temptations of life. Only the successful candidates could then at last ascend to the ruling class of the philosopher kings.

In economics we often study interactions between agents without ever engaging with them. During my PhD, I was investigating all kinds of theories and hypotheses about what firms might, could, or even should do without actually having any idea about how firms really weigh their decisions. My usual approach was to derive a set of hypotheses from some assumptions about how firms could potentially behave in some environment, without actually having a clue of what was really going on.

If we live through a certain situation, we get an understanding of how people make their respective choices, according to the situational logic they face. These choices are often fully rational, but important information on the respective situations may remain hidden, such as the relevant agents, their preferences, or the available endowments. We need to know the constraints the agents face, how they interact, and how everything plays out. Without also living through these same types of situations, this knowledge is rather difficult to obtain.

Hayek (1943) argues that the target of the social sciences is to look at the interrelated actions of men. Because we are human, too, we can try to ourselves dive into the respective situations. In the social sciences, things are what people think they are. We can easily orient ourselves in environments where we know what people think. In contrast, if we do not share the relevant knowledge with someone, we will not be able to understand the actions he or she makes in his or her environment. When we want to understand human action, we need to know what people think in their respective situations. When we say we "understand" the action of a particular person, we imply something more than the facts; we know what we would have done under these same circumstances (or we do think so at least).

The Sophist Protagoras was probably the most famous relativist in ancient Greek. Like for all pre-Socratic philosophers, we have only fragments of his thoughts left, which survived embedded in the works of later philosophers. It is thus hard to tell what Protagoras actually meant. His most famous statement is that "man is the measure of all things". The standard example philosophers use with respect to Protagoras is the difference between warm and cold, which always depends on the respective person, on the constitution of his or her body. We can objectively measure the temperature, but some persons are used to coldness, others not. Some persons are sensitive, others not. The objective measure of 5 degrees Celsius is not always helpful. Sometimes only the individual itself can tell us what is true for him or her. The perception of coldness is different for everyone. The fact of 15 degrees Celsius as such is clearly not relative, but the lesson we can draw from Protagoras is that sometimes we cannot understand human action when only objective facts are taken into consideration.

The so-called standpoint view in sociology holds that while some facts are more visible to marginalized groups, other facts are more visible to privileged groups. The same is true for the viewpoints of both practitioners and academics. Whereas a practitioner sees facts about one process from the inside, academics see facts about many processes from the outside.

By practical experience I mean people who have lived in particular work situations for several years and have sufficient knowledge to adequately abstract the most relevant aspects of their proper situation. Of those practical people, the most reflective ones inclined to reading and writing should get the chance to write a PhD thesis. They will be able to put forward an actual, and potentially original, thesis then. In case the scientific analysis sets a too high demand for technicalities, an intertwined approach may be a solution, where PhD students work only part of their time in the private sector or the government. Importantly, a mere exchange of ideas between researchers and practical people will not suffice. If one wants to have a thorough understanding of a subject, only personal experience is sufficient, as otherwise one misses out on important details and lacks a general guidance toward important, and often implicit, aspects of the subject, which accompany one throughout the project.

Economists who move from their theories to practical affairs often fail (see, e.g., the disaster of Long-Term Capital Management, as documented by Lowenstein 2001). We develop theories valid for the general, abstract situation, and these theories are almost always inadequate in the specific, detailed situation. Few economic theories give an economist in a particular business situation an advantage over an experienced practitioner, who knows his or her business, both the pros and cons. The practitioner may not always understand exactly why, but he or she certainly knows how things work.

Vice versa, one might object that practical experience can never be generalized. Yet many jobs in the private sector are different only on the surface. Humans have a tendency to react in a similar way even when the situations are very different. For example, a manager working in a specific industry has few problems transferring to another industry. Through at least some practical experience in a few different jobs, one can already learn a lot about how different people respond to incentives, how they decide, act, react, and function. The question will then be whether this knowledge is scalable, that is, whether it holds for aggregate behaviors, too, and how it alters it. This will be the research task; to map out the implications of the experience one has gathered in practice.

On the surface, the judgment of an experienced entrepreneur is only a single observation when compared to, for example, a finding based on a sample of firms. However, the entrepreneur has accumulated and meaningfully integrated countless observations over time. His judgment incorporates clearly ordered information, akin to an intelligent time series. A practitioner can thus often give a more valuable answer than a sample of firms ever could. The problem will of course be how representative the entrepreneur's time series really is. The entrepreneur usually has a lot of time variation, but relatively few cross-sectional variation (i.e., working in different firms). However, the central advantage of the entrepreneur is that he can put meaning into his surroundings; he knows what will happen.

Personal involvement in a subject also strongly increases the motivation to really understand it. Intrinsic motivation is the most decisive input into a successful search for truth. If someone has lived through a situation, she will be motivated to gain true answers to her questions, and she will only be content if she can approach truth as close as possible. If someone else gives the reasons for investigating a subject (e.g., the academic literature), the intrinsic motivation to really understand it will be much lower. To excel, the relevant questions must have popped up in the mind of the researcher by themselves; and the stronger the researcher longs for a true answer, the less distracted she will be by prestige.

The most important contribution of practical experience will be its role as a filter to prevent the creation and propagation of false feedback, and to aid in eliminating false theories and coming up with more realistic theories. In cases devoid of any reliable empirical evidence, practical experience may take its place in falsifying or corroborating economic theories. Practical experience would thus serve as a via negativa (Taleb 2012). Nonetheless, even the most insightful practical experience will never have the last word. The scientific method requires that even the very best insights emerging from practical experience have at some point to pass through rigorous empirical testing, too.

13 Robustness checks

Robustness checks are a very important element in the pursuit of true feedback. They can show whether the results of a study crucially depend on certain choices of researcher degrees of freedom or whether alternative series of choices of researcher degrees of freedom lead to similar results. However, in each robustness check, only careful thinking about whether the choices of the specific researcher degrees of freedom are appropriate can lead closer to true feedback. If the final specification turns out to be robust, but always in the direction of false feedback, we will not have gained much.

Many p-hacked specifications are robust by their very definition. Researchers often mine their data until they obtain a set of robust final specifications, implying that the results will hold up in various alternative specifications, too. The robustness checks presented in published studies are therefore often not real tests of alternative choices of researcher degrees of freedom, but rather the very reason why the researchers have chosen these particular specifications in the first place.

If a certain specification has been chosen because it is robust, it is not necessarily less likely to constitute false feedback than other possible specifications, because the most robust specification does not automatically coincide with the true way through the garden of forking paths. In fact, a specification developed from a thorough ex-ante perspective is in most instances likely to be quite different from it. Even if researchers p-hack a robust specification very carefully, they will not make less, and probably even more, wrong turns on their way back through the garden of forking paths.

Moreover, the majority of robustness checks presented in a published article constitute only minor deviations from the main specification. Some researchers excel in using large numbers of only marginally relevant robustness checks to demonstrate the alleged strength of their evidence, while those robustness checks indeed wreaking havoc with the stability of the main results are silently omitted, and if someone does indeed raise a concern, more or less elegantly discussed away. Batteries of robustness checks are thus often more of a hand waving exercise to pre-empt potential criticism.

The strongest or most significant specification usually occupies center stage in the final study. The presented robustness checks are then those alternative specifications that tend to work out as well but are generally weaker or less significant. The usual proceeding is then to argue that "even if we do X or Y, our results still hold up". Ironically, often some of these follow-up and subsidiary robustness checks would actually be much more appropriate than the main specification.

The current practice of presenting a battery of robustness checks is also severely undermined by the fact that these robustness checks practically never fail. It is hardly possible that in a published study all of the conducted robustness checks indeed hold up. True robustness checks should fail from time to time, even if these failures are just noise in the form of false negatives; the statistical power of most studies is simply not high enough to let through all of the presented robustness checks.

Robust statistical findings that pass smoothly through every possible robustness check can thus even be evidence of extensive p-hacking. An honest ex-ante approach relying on a pre-specified analysis is extremely unlikely to yield such a neat outcome. At least some of all the applied robustness checks should lead to less clean findings. The problem is of course that when researchers truthfully show their partly inconsistent results, the study will fall behind the majority of extensively p-hacked studies that repeatedly nudge everyone into an illusion of statistical perfection.

Most reviewers hardly know where the weak spots of p-hacked results are without also seeing the data. The authors will of course present those robustness checks that seem obvious from an outside perspective. And if another researcher indeed raises critical robustness checks, the authors are often quick to consciously p-hack them away, as they tend to see such externally imposed robustness checks seldom as crucial elements to their main message.

True robustness checks of a study would start out the entire way through the garden of forking paths from anew again, without the knowledge of what kind of other specifications have been tried out already. Only a fresh perspective on how to execute the empirical strategy provides a serious robustness check. Different researchers will have to analyze the context of the study and try to derive in a maximally objective manner those ways through the garden of forking paths that best approximate true feedback.

14 Replication

14.1 A defense

The key requirement for publication in economics is that your contribution is novel, that is, your study needs to be sufficiently different from the existing literature. Each study is somehow assumed to have proven the effect of an empirical strategy in a given context conclusively. New studies can at most complement or extend previous studies, but, ideally, they investigate something else entirely. The setup of each new study has to be sufficiently different from the setup of all previous studies; one cannot improve previous studies by replicating them, otherwise the study will not be novel enough. Each new study will then, of course, itself conclusively prove the effect of the applied empirical strategy in a given context. While this heavy focus on the novel makes sense in theoretical economics, it is counterproductive in empirical economics. To tackle the issues surrounding excessive researcher degrees of freedom, we would need to be able to directly compare alternative studies taking place in a given context. Otherwise, we cannot asses the influence of all the various alternative ways through the garden of forking paths. If all studies are always required to be different from each other, we cannot adequately compare them and have no means to assess the influence of variation in researcher degrees of freedom on the findings. To draw reliable conclusions about the literature in a field, we need maximal comparability between individual studies, otherwise we cannot separate corroborating and falsifying empirical evidence and make adequate judgments about which of them weighs heavier.

Ideally, a culture of replication would bring us more empirical studies focusing on our most important economic hypotheses and less empirical studies focusing on the manifold of minor variations around these most important hypotheses. The false feedback produced by the latter merely clouds assessment of the relevant literature, while the false feedback produced by the former is even desired, as it provides numerous different estimates through which we can collectively test our most important economic hypotheses.

Most of the contributions we deem as novel are far from being truly novel. They are only variations of the very same exemplar studies we are already familiar with. The truly novel has a hard time to establish itself. While we always want to see novel things, those novel things also need to closely resemble what we are already used to. To be successful, novelty needs to come in small doses. Every now and then, however, truly novel studies win out the day and position themselves as the new exemplar studies in a field around which other researchers can then center their own contributions; they apply similar ideas on similar topics. At the same time, however, these supposedly novel contributions are too different from each other to allow for an adequate comparison between them. The large majority of our studies are thus trapped somewhere in the space between truly novel contributions and unsystematic variation around these truly novel contributions. Instead of producing a constant stream of contributions that are novel only on the surface, we would better focus our efforts on getting those truly novel exemplar studies right. We would need to pursue systematic and meaningful variation around these most important studies, such that we obtain evidence about their strengths and weaknesses. The better such an exemplar study is, the more effort and scrutiny we should invest into it.

Quantifying economic effects in the most exact and reliable is absolute key to achieve scientific progress. Without correctly estimated effect sizes we cannot reliably build on past work. It can make a huge difference to know whether an effect is positive or whether an effect is positive but small or positive but large. Knowledge of only the direction of an effect leaves open all kinds of speculation about its potential impact. Precise knowledge of the size of an effect, on the other hand, makes it possible to judge how relevant it is and how it compares to other effects. Without knowledge of the size of an effect, an ordering of its importance with respect to other effects is hardly feasible.

The first step in this is to make transparent which effects show more and which show less variation due to the garden of forking paths. In other words, we have to quantify the methodological uncertainty about the feedback we obtain. Only in some cases the different estimates will converge toward a specific effect size over time. However, knowledge about which effects vary due to the garden of forking paths and which do not is very valuable, as it implies that we do not yet know enough about either the theoretical or empirical mechanisms leading to the observed findings.

Sample variation alone can let estimates vary considerably. To provide estimates of the uncertainty caused by statistical noise, researcher could rely more often on confidence intervals; a graphical illustration of confidence intervals gives a good impression about this type of uncertainty. The use of confidence intervals is probably still limited because they often imply way too large intervals, which may in turn undermine the credibility of the study in the eyes of other researchers. One can hide much uncertainty through illusory dichotomous distinctions of significant versus not significant.

Large effects with few confounders are in general much easier to detect and are thus also more likely to already have been detected. Many of the low-hanging fruits in empirical economics have already been picked. The novel effects we can still detect are mostly smaller effects with more confounders. This reasoning implies that the quality of the empirical evidence tends to decline over time (Gelman and Carlin 2014). Even though methodology may lead to continuous progress, later empirical studies aim at targets that wobble around way more. The result will be even more false feedback, mostly likely in the form of gross overestimations (Gelman and Carlin 2014). Consequently, it would make sense to focus our efforts on improved estimates of the existing large and thus relevant effects than repeatedly fail to exactly estimate new but small and thus also more irrelevant effects.

An effect is real only when it is replicable, when one can independently observe it in alternative contexts. Yet a single study can only examine a subset of the variation in the garden of forking paths. Nonetheless, researchers seldom limit their inference to precisely the paths taken. If a scientific result should reveal a regularity about the world, it needs to generalize to other ways in the garden of forking paths, too. To find out to which ways the result generalizes over is the task of replication (Nosek and Errington 2020a). If the replication study pursues systematic variation of relevant forking paths, successful replication provides evidence that the result generalizes to a wider space of forking paths, whereas unsuccessful replication indicates that the result does not generalize beyond the specific forking paths already taken; the result is more constrained. The pursuit of replications clears the picture about the generalizability of a result. It contributes to identifying the conditions necessary for the emergence of it (Nosek and Errington 2020a). Each replication improves our theoretical understanding of the result. The way in which results vary with the garden of forking paths can deliver valuable new insights. Replication is therefore most promising when we have only a rough understanding about a given finding. Each replication can inform us further about the extent of its applicability. Nosek and Errington (2020a) argue that outcomes from replication are ingredients for "refining, altering, or extending theory". Replicable evidence provides an anchor for the development of better theories.

Even a direct replication does not need to be an exact copy of the original study. Rather, a direct replication must redo the essential features of the original study (Zwaan et al. 2018). It needs to make the same choices of theoretically or contextually important researcher degrees of freedom. The original study must describe the conditions necessary for the emergence of the effect. Every published study must contain all elements that allow independent researchers to replicate it. All consequential researcher degrees of freedom must be defined, and only those researcher degrees of freedom deemed inconsequential can be omitted (Zwaan et al. 2018). If the respective context fails the replication, and researchers find a crucial auxiliary hypothesis, they can investigate it in a new study. Should the study confirm it, we have increased the explanatory power of the theory (Zwaan et al. 2018).

The most promising strategy to publish a study is not just a novel finding but an as surprising, unexpected, or counterintuitive finding as possible. Unfortunately, unexpected hypotheses generally have a much lower post-study probability of being true than more straightforward hypotheses, even if the empirical evidence in line with them seems strong. The probability of a hypotheses to be true may sound esoteric to non-Bayesians. A hypothesis is either true or it is not. It is more intuitive in, for example, studies of genome associations, as described in Ioannidis (2005). When among hundreds of thousands of gene polymorphisms only a handful can have an effect on schizophrenia, and none of them has any special standing in having an effect on it, the pre-study probability of each individual polymorphism is extremely low. In such a setting, one could, for instance, assign each gene polymorphism a prior probability of one divided by the total number of all gene polymorphisms. In economics, in contrast, it would be rather hard to assign prior probabilities to some hypotheses, even if you bought into Bayesian thinking. It would cause a huge debate about which hypotheses would be more probable ex-ante, and the ranking would vary enormously depending on the respective researcher. Nonetheless, the Bayesian way provides interesting avenues for thinking about the strength of evidence.

The pre-study probability that a hypothesis is true is crucial for its post-study probability to be true. The lower the ratio of true relationships to no relationships, the lower is the probability that a statistically significant finding is indeed true, even in an otherwise perfect experiment. Colquhoun (2014, 2017) illustrates this point with numerical examples. He considers an unbiased experiment with an adequate power of 0.8 but an ex-ante unlikely hypothesis. Imagine, for instance, a large-scale experiment trying to show that humans do intentionally and systematically not respond to incentives. Suppose this experiment has produced a p-value of exactly 0.01. How likely is it then that the alternative hypothesis is indeed true? To approximate this, we can make use of Bayes' theorem. For instance, if the pre-study probability of the null hypothesis is 0.9, the null hypothesis is nine times more likely than the alternative hypothesis. In this setting, a p-value of exactly 0.01 corresponds to a post-study probability of 0.37 that the null hypothesis is indeed true. This is considerably higher than the common threshold of a false-positive risk of 0.05 would demand. The supposedly strong evidence of p = 0.01 in line with the alternative hypothesis is not sufficient to turn around the high pre-study probability of the null hypothesis of 0.9. Hence, even for an otherwise perfect experiment, running tests of unlikely hypotheses incur a high probability that the ones for which we find evidence are still false.

The strength of evidence a p-value lends to a hypothesis can thus be low, especially if the pre-study probability of it being true is low. Many researchers tend to confuse the p-value with the probability that a hypothesis is true. However, the p-value only gives information about how compatible the data are with the statistical model, it is not a measure of truth of the tested hypothesis (see, e.g., Wasserstein and Lazar 2016). The p-value is the probability of obtaining data at least as extreme if the null hypothesis and all the assumptions of the statistical model are true. The probability of a hypothesis to be true depends on several factors, namely its pre-study probability to be true, the type I and type II errors, and the degree of twisting of the econometric model (see, e.g., Ioannidis 2005). If we want to obtain estimates about the probability of a hypothesis to be true, we need Bayesian thinking.

Bettis (2012) argues that a true null hypothesis that turns out statistically significant is by a perverse logic more likely to constitute an interesting or counter-intuitive result. A false positive may be very interesting simply because the null hypothesis is actually true and that therefore the effect does not, in fact, exist. One did rightfully not expect ex-ante to observe this unlikely positive result.

Ironically, an increased focus on eliminating false positives may also lead to an increase in false negatives. Researchers may shy away from improbable hypotheses and concentrate on what is more probable. Yet to achieve scientific progress, a small set of solid answers is much more valuable than a large set of mostly false answers, especially if we have difficulties in discriminating between the two.

The task of empirical researchers is not to be maximally creative. Our task should be to conduct studies that approach true feedback as close as possible. If this means that we have to repeat similar exercises over and over again, so be it. Economics as a science does not profit from excessive creativity that produces endless instances of false feedback. Creativity is key when we face clearly defined empirical puzzles. However, amid false feedback, we do not even know whether we indeed face such puzzles or not. Discussion of the same questions again and again is also not necessarily a bad thing. There will always be enough perspectives to ensure a vivid exchange between theory and empirics. For instance, many questions in philosophy have been discussed for more than 2500 years now, without making them any less interesting. According to Popper (1959), scientific progress is the replacement of old theories through new theories providing a better fit to empirical reality. In the same manner, we have to search for those ways through the garden of forking paths that best approximate true feedback. Discussing the same problems again and again is not futile, but an essential ingredient to progress. We do not need different, but better answers to these same questions we keep asking.

Whereas a study that cannot adequately respond to concerns raised in a replication loses some of the confidence in its results, a study that withstands these concerns gains additional confidence in its results. While replication is time consuming for both sides, it helps the research community better understand the shortfalls and merits of the underlying study and whether it should be taken less or more seriously. The usual dilemma is reversed: the costs are private and the gains are socialized.

The number of successful replications of a given study could even develop into a signal of the strength of a study. The higher the ratio of successful versus unsuccessful replications, the more reliable the study is. The amount of replication efforts invested into a given study would show the degree of interest it sparks among the research community, and authors should be proud of it. The best studies would pass repeated attempts at falsification. A study that has never replicated will never gain such a reputation. Studies that have never been replicated would be looked at with more suspicion.

Researchers need to be concerned with why studies differ from each other. We need to investigate why different replication attempts lead to different results. Without finding explanations for why studies differ from each other, we will never be able to understand the causes behind the false feedback we produce. We need to be able to pin down the central sources of false feedback. This we can only achieve through a sensible comparison of large numbers of studies designed to be maximally comparable to each other, and, in the ideal case, with controlled variation of important sources of false feedback.

Once replication studies have identified how an effect varies due to the garden of forking paths, we can go on and show how it varies with the environment. Only after we have gained an understanding of the impact of the garden of forking paths, we can move on to understand how an effect varies with the environment. If we continue to pool the two, the difficulties in our understanding will remain, as we will not be able to discriminate between variation due to the garden of forking paths and variation due to the environment.

Repeated replication will be most needed for those hypotheses that are of high economic relevance but the economics profession nevertheless strongly disagrees about. Priority should be on the elimination of false theories, such that we can discard of baggage. To achieve this, we need to replicate our empirical studies in a myriad of ways, until we possess reliable evidence enabling us to judge whether a theory is indeed falsified or not.

14.2 Transparency

In large and complex projects, learning from the data is often inevitable and sometimes even necessary. In such projects, it is impossible to foresee all the steps until the final analysis, because too many unexpected situations will occur and the researchers have to deviate from what they have planned initially. Systematic screening of the data can refute wrong priors that would have led the project into the wrong direction right from the outset. During every large and complex project, researchers plot thousands of graphs, calculate thousands of descriptive statistics, and run thousands of estimations. Good empirical researchers watch the data closely, try to understand it, and then fit their specifications accordingly. Otherwise, research would be inefficient, every wrong prior would require its own study. However, the entire work process on such a project, every major trial and also every major error, would need to be adequately documented and openly visible to others. This lack of maximal transparency in applied research is one of the central problems; only few researchers pursue specification searching openly.

To increase transparency, researchers should provide access to the data and codes they employed in their analyses. Many journals have already enforced this practice with exceptions granted for proprietary data (which is a problem of its own, as none or only few researchers can verify such studies). Unfortunately, the data and codes uploaded to journal webpages are often unstructured and incomplete. The authors would need to make sure that their data and code files allow for reproduction of their results, which will force them to be transparent in every step of the econometric analysis and also to check for potential errors. Authors have to show openly the potential weak spots of their analyses. The studies need skin in the game, the possibility to fall due to relevant criticism.

Sometimes we will even have to pursue the tedious exercise of collecting the raw data again and redo the countless silent steps that were made in cleaning and processing the raw data, because many researchers only send the final versions of their datasets on which they have run their final specifications. This hides silent steps performed during the collecting, cleaning, and processing stages.

There exist two types of empirical researchers: those who are especially careful with their research project when they know others will probably never see it, and those who are especially careful with their research project when they know others will probably see it. We need to reward the former type of empirical researchers accordingly, and only a broad move toward transparency can do so.

An airplane manufacturer does not market a new airplane and simply assume that no one will look too closely whether it is indeed capable of flying without repeated crashes. In order for airlines to buy it, the manufacturer must be maximally transparent. If the airplane design contains mistakes (as it happened with the software of Boeing 737 Max), trust erodes quickly, and no one will buy.

Even simple reproduction of economic studies is not always guaranteed. Gertler et al. (2018) collect 203 empirical articles not containing proprietary or restricted data published in nine leading economics journals in May 2016. They are able to reproduce final tables and figures in 37% of cases, while in just 14% of cases they can do the same starting from the raw data. Similarly, Chang and Li (2017) replicate 67 published macroeconomic articles from 13 well-regarded journals using author-provided data and code files. They can replicate the results of only about half of articles. Chang and Li (2017) also find that if both code and data were not openly available beforehand, due to the requirements set by the journals, the rate of successful reproduction of studies is much lower.

To combat this low reproducibility, the American Economic Association (AEA) appointed a data editor for its journals on January 2018 (Vilhuber 2019). The main task of the data editor is to assure that the data and code of the studies published in the AEA journals are openly available and allow for reproduction of results. The enforcement of the policy remains with the editor responsible for the study though. Problems arise with restricted-access data, for which it remains difficult to verify whether they allow for a reproduction of the results in the study. This move of the AEA goes exactly into the right direction. It sets a standard that other journals will have to follow in the future.

Over recent years, there has already been a movement toward open science practices in the social sciences. Christensen et al. (2020) investigate this movement through the State of Social Science (S3) survey, which measures attitudes, norms, and adoption toward open science in a broadly representative sample of researchers from economics, political sciences, psychology, and sociology. They document a steep increase in the adoption of open science practices such as posting data, code, and materials as well as in preregistering studies, hypotheses, and analyses in all four disciplines over the last years. Moreover, they find a high level of support toward open science practices. Christensen et al. (2020) even argue that the social sciences are experiencing a scientific paradigm shift toward open science. Such increased transparency paves the way for future efforts to close in on true feedback.

However, open data and codes will merely show that the final specifications as described in the study are reproducible. It never shows how many estimations it took researchers to get there. Most important, it does not resolve the problem that the way chosen through the garden of forking paths may be quite far from the true path. The only test for this would be if several independent researchers came up with the same decisions for the most important researcher degrees of freedom.

14.3 Exploration and confirmation

Leamer (1978) tells us the following story:

> I began thinking about these problems when I was a graduate student in economics at the University of Michigan, 1966–1970. At that time there was a very active group building an econometric model of the United States. As it happens, the econometric modeling was done in the basement of the building and the econometric theory courses were taught on the top floor (the third). I was perplexed by the fact that the same language was used in both places. Even more amazing was the transmogrification of particular individuals who wantonly sinned in the basement and metamorphosed into the highest of high priests as they ascended to the third floor.

If people were secretly p-hacking in the 1970s and still do so today, they will probably continue so for the few next decades ahead.

One solution to deal with p-hacking is to adequately designate its results as such. Wagenmakers et al. (2012) demand a clear distinction between exploratory and confirmatory studies. Researchers can rely on existing data to generate theories, but to test theories they need new data. Exploratory research can give indications about a hypothesis, but since it may just fit patterns of statistical noise, to test the hypothesis researchers need new data not containing these same patterns of statistical noise. In exploratory studies, researchers can mine their data as much as they want, as long as they explicitly present the obtained findings as only tentative. In confirmatory studies, in contrast, researchers execute an ex-ante planned research design and data analysis that does not alter once the realized data are observed. This prevents the empirical analysis from merely overfitting statistical noise.

The straightforward solution to draw such a line between exploratory and confirmatory research is a pre-analysis plan that details both the study design and the ensuing data analysis (see, e.g., Nosek et al. 2018). A pre-analysis plan requires researchers to commit to analytic steps before they observe any outcomes in their data. The commitment becomes credible through registration of the pre-analysis plan in an independent registry, such as the website www.socialscienceregistry.org, the registry for randomized controlled trials of the American Economic Association, which provides every pre-analysis plan with a timestamp. The more detailed a pre-analysis plan is, the more credible the study will be, as it decreases the space for possible ex-post analytical choices of the researchers.

This clear division between exploratory and confirmatory research approaches the scientific ideal quite well. Not only does it guarantee that an empirical analysis does not overfit the data, it also allows for systematic improvements of theory. If researchers commit to a certain theory and lay out a detailed way to test it and, in light of the data, the theory proves inadequate, because, for instance, the data refute some key aspect of the theory, exploratory research can investigate possible reasons for the refutations. The pre-analysis plans of any follow-up studies can then incorporate possible corrections or adjustments of the theory. This would allow theory to progress in a maximally transparent, albeit rather slow, way.

However, pre-analysis plans are not free from concerns either. If the adherence to the pre-analysis plan is not enforced, researchers can freely deviate from it. Detailed pre-analysis plans containing a timestamp make such deviations easily visible though. Other researchers can directly compare the final study with the pre-analysis plan, which will highlight any switch from confirmatory to exploratory analysis. In some instances, deviations from the pre-analysis plan can make perfect sense. For example, if there is a problem with the data that could not possibly have been foreseen. On the other hand, if, for instance, the main outcome variable is substituted with an alternative variable, alarm bells should go off. Nonadherence may even include the storyline of the final article. Researchers could run the analysis as planned but emphasize only those findings that work. A detailed pre-analysis plan, where the main story of the study is clearly defined, would inhibit such deviations.

Unfortunately, depositing a pre-analysis plan only makes sense if the researcher has not yet seen the data, such as in randomized controlled trials, where the data collection will take place in the future. In observational studies, in contrast, where the data are already in circulation, deposition of a pre-analysis plan is often not credible, as researchers can simply p-hack their data ex-ante and then select their preferred set of specifications for deposition in the registry.

Preregistration of observational studies might be interesting for prospective events though; for instance, the effects of an upcoming event, such as an important policy change, on certain economic outcomes. The prediction of the economic consequences of such prospective events offers an ideal setup for the potential falsification or corroboration of a given theory. Journals could even dedicate special issues including independent teams to the systematic analysis of such prospective events.

Neumark (2001) presents an example for this promising type of pre-registration. He observes that authors in the minimum wage literature may have made model specification decisions that tend to systematically push results into a certain direction. To combat this problem of "author effects", Neumark (2001) pre-specified a research design well before new data on minimum wages and employment became publicly available. He then submitted the pre-specified research design for peer review and applied this reviewed version of the research design on the data, after it had finally been made publicly available. Such a preregistration allows for the incorporation of opposing perspectives of researchers into the empirical strategy. The participating researchers have to commit to an empirical strategy before even seeing the data and specification searches and thus also potential author effects pushing the data into a certain direction become impossible.

This particular format is called "registered reports" (Chambers 2019). These are pre-analysis plans peer reviewed by other researchers, who assess the quality of the described research question, theory, and methods. The back and forth between authors and reviewers takes place before the study is executed. Once a registered report is accepted, it implies that the study will be published, irrespective of its outcome. The authors then carry out the study and a second stage of the review process starts, in which reviewers can again make comments. However, their comments should focus only on whether the authors adhered to the registered report. Hardwicke and Ioannidis (2018) name three advantages of registered reports. First, the review of the report before the onset of the study can help to detect flaws in its design. Second, because acceptance is based only on the question and methodology, and not on the results, it allows for insignificant or untidy results. Third, the protocol is under supervision of the editors and the reviewers, which increase the need for adherence to it.

How spread are pre-analysis plans in economics? Abrams et al. (2020) assess the registry for RCTs of the AEA, with sobering results. They find that over 90% of RCTs do not register. This rate is lower in top journals though: about half of the RCTs published in top journals between 2017 and 2019 have indeed registered. Overall, of those RCTs that register, only half have registered before the intervention began. Moreover, roughly 90% of studies do not provide information beyond the minimal categories required at registration. Note that the AEA registry does not require the deposition of a pre-analysis plan, which is in general much more detailed than the categories required by mere registration. Consequently, only 11% of submissions contained a pre-analysis plan. Abrams et al. (2020) argue that the information provided by the preregistered RCTs is in the majority of cases not sufficient to significantly aid inference. The entries in the AEA registry are too unspecific and still allow for way too much discretionary room. Abrams et al. (2020) therefore conclude their investigation by stating that there is only limited progress toward solving the file drawer problem and p-hacking.

Pre-analysis plans cannot solve the problem that there may be numerous alternative ways through the garden of forking paths that are more adequate. By choosing an ex-ante path through the garden of forking paths, they can rule out most ex-post choices of researcher degrees of freedom and thus guarantee more valid p-values, but they cannot solve the problem of false choices. By sticking to one series of forking paths, they disregard alternative specifications that may in fact be more adequate; the pre-analysis plan may therefore describe a false way through the garden of forking paths. The p-values can deliver correct inference for the wrong statistical model.

Moreover, pre-analysis plans do not restrict the problem of variation in feedback. Taking a pre-specified way through the garden of forking paths does not diminish the wide array of alternative, equally reasonable ways that might have led to very different results. Only if the garden of forking paths is laid out as a whole we can make judgments about how estimates vary, and thus narrow down the extent of variation in feedback. Otherwise, obtaining a certain outcome depends on luck; the researchers have picked this particular path by mere accident, and various counterfactual paths not taken may in fact contradict the outcome.

14.4 Repeated replication

As outlined in Section 14.1, the main solution to the problem of false feedback is repeated replication. We need to rethink, compare, and replicate our most important studies, again and again, accompanied by constructive discussions about how to exactly conduct the ideal replications of each study and how to set conditions for falsification. Replication makes only sense if the studies are credible in the first place, that is, if they offer a chance at uncovering true feedback. Some correlational analysis might prove highly replicable, yet if it is also highly endogenous, we will likely not have gained much useful insights. The target of each replication exercise is to obtain an estimate of the variance of feedback centered around those forking paths that approach true feedback best. If a series of estimates point consistently into the wrong direction, we might indeed be able to precisely estimate the variance around the obtained feedback, but it will move us backward and not forward. Thus, if we only have a set of highly endogenous correlations, discussion about potentially superior ways through the garden of forking paths will be futile. In contrast, replicating our most important studies could break with many of the false feedback bubbles we are currently in and introduce what we actually need: repeated measurements of the same hidden structures of economic reality, hopefully converging toward true feedback over time.

We can divide efforts for replication into four levels of increasing stringency. First, and most obvious, researchers should subject studies to additional robustness checks to rule out the possibility that the estimates depend crucially on some arbitrary auxiliary hypotheses. This allows detecting those instances where researchers misuse the totality of their researcher degrees of freedom to produce fragile estimates satisfying their desired outcome criteria. Second, researchers need to vary the ways through the garden of forking paths in a sensible manner. The main target of a replication is always to pursue an as true series of forking paths as possible; the methodological decisions need to be adequate. To investigate instances where adequate decisions are difficult to make, researchers could rely on methods to report large numbers of different results, such as "specification curve" (Simonsohn et al. 2020) or "multiverse analysis" (Steegen et al. 2016). Each independent replication could provide its preferred set of estimates, and the more such alternative estimates we have, the clearer the overall picture becomes. Third, promising studies will have to be replicated on new or unused data originating from the same or similar environments. This is key to address the issue that p-hacked empirical evidence did not yet pass attempts at falsification. The use of new data makes it possible to subject the studies to statistical tests with adequate significance thresholds. Fourth, we need replications on datasets from new environments. Instead of relying on the estimate from the same or similar environments, these replications could show how the estimates change with variation in time and place.

Clemens (2017) provides a standard that divides different forms of replications into four categories. He argues that current terminology, which groups every attempt to redo the insights of a study under the term replication, leads to much confusion. Clemens (2017) defines "replication" more narrowly as attempts to show whether under the same conditions a study can achieve the same results. Replication can take on two forms: i) verification and ii) reproduction. Whereas a verification applies the same specification, the same population, and the same sample, a reproduction applies the same specification and the same population but uses a different sample. In contrast, Clemens (2017) defines "robustness" more broadly as attempts to show how a study varies under different conditions. Robustness can also take on two forms: iii) reanalysis and iv) extension. Whereas a reanalysis applies a different specification, it relies on the same population and the same sample. Finally, an extension applies the same specification but uses a different population and sample. Whether the standard of Clemens (2017) is the last answer remains open. However, how exactly we group replications will prove crucial, as passing one level does not provide the same level of credibility as passing through all four levels.

Of course, observational studies, which form the core of empirical economics, cannot be repeated deliberately many times like it is possible in the case of experiments. We can therefore often not replicate studies using different samples from the same population (except for sample splits or subsamples). In contrast, there should be sufficient data available to test the same hypothesis in alternative contexts, such as different economies or different times. This type of replication is certainly much more demanding. Yet if independent replications of a given study deliver similar results across many different contexts, this can send a very powerful message.

Because good natural experiments do not necessarily happen repeatedly and in many different contexts, we require approaches that allow us profiting the most from the few good opportunities we have. The only way to investigate the credibility of good natural experiments is thus reanalysis. For this, we need tools that allow analyzing these rare opportunities in a broad way.

Ideally, the authors of the original study continue to present the way through the garden of forking paths which they think is most appropriate; that is, the specifications they think approach true feedback best. The researchers replicating the study should then have the opportunity to double-check the applied specifications, and, if necessary, present alternative ways through the garden of forking paths they consider as more appropriate.

The specification curve of Simonsohn et al. (2020) and the multiverse analysis of Steegen et al. (2016) present tools that could greatly facilitate any debate about which ways through the garden of forking paths is best. They are intuitive implementations of Leamer's (1978, 1983, 1985) vision of a sensitivity analysis and are able to show the large space of potentially "whimsical" choices researchers can make. Both specification curve and multiverse analysis allow simultaneously reporting the results of thousands of reasonable alternative specifications in a highly aggregated way. Their compactness makes it possible to show much wider variation in researcher degrees of freedom than would ever be possible within the confines of standard robustness checks. Simonsohn et al. (2020) define reasonable specifications as: i) sensible tests of the research question, ii) expected to be statistically valid, iii) not redundant with other specifications in the set. Both specification curve and multiverse analysis allow comparing all types of researcher degrees of freedom, not just control variables, but also estimation methods, functional forms, outliers, or measurement of variables. When the set of reasonable specifications becomes too large, a possible solution is to estimate a random subset of a few thousand specifications (Simonsohn et al. 2020). The graphical representation of forking paths that is part of the two methods allows identifying those researcher degrees of freedom responsible for large variation in results. The simultaneous comparison of forking paths also enables carving out the respective methodological stance of the different researchers more clearly. Both methods cannot necessarily settle disagreements between researchers, especially if they have fundamentally different theoretical perspectives. To settle such conflicts, we would need to improve the ground upon which we stand. That is, we would need better theories that connect the different perspectives and dissolve the disagreements (Simonsohn et al. 2020). In the same vein, if we cannot come to a conclusion about which set of forking paths should be preferred even within the same theoretical perspective, we will have to deflate the entire multiverse of specifications by making theory more precise and more complete (Steegen et al. 2016). In both instances, specification curve and multiverse analysis can greatly help in shedding light on eventual disagreements. They allow isolating whether differences in results depend on theoretically important or on more arbitrary choices of researcher degrees of freedom. Importantly, if the majority of forking paths displayed by the two methods show large p-values, we can only conclude that the data are not sufficient to draw reliable inferences; the uncertainty present in the data remains too high.

As discussed in the previous section, pre-analysis plans cannot address that the particular way taken through the garden of forking paths may only be one way among a great many others. There may exist alternative, equally reasonable series of forking paths delivering very different results. Whereas pre-analysis plans can protect against p-hacking, they cannot shed light on the multiverse of forking paths. To combat this problem, researchers could combine pre-analysis plan with multiverse analysis. They could specify and single out in advance all reasonable forking paths and then conduct the much broader multiverse analysis. Such a combination would harvest the benefits of both approaches; the pre-analysis plan would assure that the researchers did not discard crucial forking paths ex-post, while the multiverse analysis allows covering a broad range of alternative forking paths.

A possible strategy to test the stability of p-hacked theoretical insights *within* a given study is a series of tests based on predictions from these same theoretical insights. If researchers have discovered an interesting pattern in their data, they could test whether it moves in line with theoretically relevant moderators. If the moderating variables change the results into the theoretically predicted direction, the researchers might indeed have hit upon a valuable theoretical insight. Of course, in practice, researchers could simply omit unsuccessful moderators and only present those moderators that tend to work. Consequently, if there is a possibility to test for theoretically motivated moderators, and the study itself did not already do it, other researchers could pursue it in a replication attempt.

In the same vein, journals in economics often require that authors apply, within the same study, the same identification strategy on different datasets or different identification strategies on the same dataset. This is a very valuable check for the impact of the garden of forking paths. However, to combat incentives for authors to present only the consistent results, it would be very preferable to let this task be performed by other, independent researchers in replication attempts.

When researchers use alternative identification strategies to target the same causal effect, they are generally not considered as replications anymore. Yet this should only be the final step in addressing a certain causal effect. Before we can move to generalizations of feedback over studies using different identification strategies, we have to shed light on the variation in feedback within the individual studies, as we need to know to which degree we can rely on them. Otherwise, we retain the large between study variation in feedback without any insights into the within study variation.

How many replication studies do we currently have in economics? Mueller-Langer et al. (2019) find that from the 126,505 studies published in top 50 economics journals between 1974 and 2014 only 130 were replication studies. This is a fraction of only 0.10% of all studies. They categorize a study as a replication when the main purpose is to test the reliability of a previously published study. By only looking at published replications in top journals, they exclude publications in lower-ranked journals, working papers, and informal replications such as students performing them in class. The problem of the latter categories is of course their much lower visibility. Mueller-Langer et al. (2019) thus underestimate the actual extent of replication in economics. Nonetheless, a fraction of only 0.10% of all studies published in top 50 journals is extremely low and not nearly sufficient to verify findings.

The only fully verifiable empirical tests in economics are experiments. The central advantage of experiments is not just that they can offer in principle maximally clean identification of treatment effects but that they can be done again, many times if necessary. If experiments are not replicated, though, we miss out on one of their central strengths. We forgo the unique opportunity experiments offer to adequately address the problems caused by excessive researcher degrees of freedom.

What is the extent of replication of experiments in economics then? Sukhtankar (2017) investigates the extent of replication in the development economics literature, which has a comparatively large share of RCTs. He includes every study with an "O" JEL classification published in a top ten economic journal between 2000 and 2015. Of the 1390 papers, 120 are RCTs and 1019 are empirical studies not involving RCTs. Sukhtankar (2017) then searches for published papers or working papers that replicated these studies, which yield 12.5% (15) replicated RCTs and 5.5% (56) replicated other empirical studies. Only about half of those (6.2% and 3.3%) have been published. The majority of the replications involves a reanalysis using alternative econometric specifications or reconfigurations of data. None pursues a replication of the exact same study on a different sample of the population. Importantly, only one published replication wholeheartedly confirmed the findings of the original study. Similarly, Maniadis et al. (2017) document the extent of replication of experimental studies in 150 economic top journals over the period 1975 to 2014. They find that about 4.2% of the experimental studies published in these 150 journals contain replications, of which about half are implicit replications that are not explicitly designated as such in the published studies. Thus, even for experimental studies, which would be ideally suited for it, replications are not a widespread practice.

Even seemingly strong experimental findings can disintegrate in replication studies. Nosek et al. (2012) tell us how they themselves were unable to replicate their own findings. In a study with 1979 online participants, Nosek and Motyl found that politically more moderate participants perceived shades of grey more accurately than more extreme participants on both the political left and right. Their statistical significance test showed a p-value of 0.01. Since Nosek and Motyl ran their study through a web browser, and data collection was very easy, they decided to run a direct replication with a sample of 1300 online participants. This gave them a power of 0.995 to detect an effect of the size of the previous study at a 0.05 significance threshold. Even though in the previous study they had not engaged in explicit p-hacking, the statistical significance of their finding vanished in the replication, with a p-value of 0.59. While the replication did not provide conclusive evidence that their initial finding was false, it generated high uncertainty about it, such that the authors refrained from its publication. One wonders how many other experimental findings could disintegrate in this same way.

Serious efforts for large-scale replication have already taken place in psychology. Take, for example, the very influential study of the Open Science Collaboration (2015), which showed that in a total of 97 experimental and correlational studies in psychology only 47% of the original effect sizes were located within the 95% confidence interval of the replicated effect sizes. This study of the Open Science Collaboration was a significant factor behind the ensuing replication crisis in psychology.

Most relevant for our context are the "Many Labs" Replication Projects of Klein et al. (2014, 2018), which also target psychology studies. These crowdsourcing projects pursue the one hypothesis and many studies approach that seems so promising in approaching true feedback. Klein et al. (2018) replicate 28 classic and contemporary published findings in psychology. They can rely on 125 different samples comprising 15,305 participants from all around the world. Only 15 of the 28 replicated studies "provided evidence of a statistically significant finding in the same direction as the original finding". Importantly, 11 of the replication studies show significant heterogeneity in the estimated effect sizes, especially when the effect sizes are larger. Thus, even though Klein et al. (2018) fixed the procedural characteristics in their replications attempts, there were still some steps hidden within the setup of the experiments that turned out to play a role. Crowdsourcing projects are therefore a formidable tool for eliciting true feedback, as they can identify variation through alternative forking paths.

If we have many replicated trials aimed at uncovering the very same true feedback, we can move to methods such as meta-analysis. Currently, researchers conducting meta-analysis in economics have to rely on very dissimilar studies from which we know that many of them correspond to false feedback. A meta-analysis of studies will thus not produce very useful insights. The differences between the setups of the individual studies are in most instances too large, as the studies are explicitly designed to always measure something different, and we tend to compare apples with pears.

There exist methods to correct meta-analysis for publication bias, that is, for the file drawer effect of missing null results (see, e.g., Andrews and Kasey 2019 or Stanley and Doucouliagos 2014). However, these methods cannot adequately address the garden of forking paths. The problem lies mainly within the existing studies themselves, with too many of them corresponding to false feedback. And if the studies themselves are problematic, no statistical method can recover true estimates.

Every meta-analysis contains covariates to control for between-study differences. Yet these covariates are not nearly sufficient to capture everything of relevance. In fact, one could ask for as many covariates as there are differences in researcher degrees of freedom in theory, design, collection, processing, or analysis of the respective studies. We need to narrow down these differences first to make sensible comparisons possible. Otherwise, meta-analysis incurs even more possibilities for specification searching than any of those underlying studies meta-analysis should help organizing.

Meta-analysis should thus build on replication studies, as they offer the ground for adequate comparisons. An important area of future research will be how we can best compare studies emerging from alternative types of replication. We will have to work out which type of replication varies how, how replications are related to each other, and how to produce a synthesis of their findings.

McShane et al. (2019b) describe how large-scale replication projects could help assessing the influence of differences in methodological choices on studies that are targeted at testing the very same hypothesis. Different large-scale replication projects in psychology have shown that the influence of methodological choices is nontrivial even in the case of only one hypothesis and many replications. McShane et al. (2019b) suggest that meta-analysis of replications should apply hierarchical modeling to allow for partial pooling of the individual studies. Importantly, assessing how differences between the replications affect the results could help isolating the influence of variation in the garden of forking paths on the obtained estimates.

Large-scale replication projects relying on replications are more difficult to pursue in economics because, once again, we are commonly bound to observational data. The crowdsourcing initiatives of Silberzahn and Uhlmann (2015) and Silberzahn et al. (2018) provide a potential solution to this problem. Replication projects could send out a dataset with a well-identified natural experiment to many different researchers. Their subsequent analysis would then allow quantifying the variation in the chosen empirical strategies and findings. Silberzahn et al. (2018) argue that "crowdsourced projects will leverage skills, perspectives, and approaches to data analysis that no single analyst or research team can realistically muster alone".

Repeated instances of thorough replication of our most promising studies will increase our chances at uncovering true feedback. The main criterion will always be that, if all fingers point into the same direction, we can have confidence that we are on the right track. John Maynard Keynes (1940) raised this crucial point already at the very beginning of modern econometrics. He referred to the legend that the seventy translators of the Septuagint were locked up with the Hebrew text in seventy separate rooms and, miraculously, emerged from these rooms with seventy identical Greek translations. Keynes doubted that if seventy econometricians were shut up with the same statistical materials, they would emerge with the very same results. However, if we shut up seventy econometricians, providing them with a well-identified research design, and sixty of these seventy econometricians emerged with qualitatively similar results, we may indeed have hit onto true feedback.

14.5 Incentives

Open discussions about whether published studies have indeed applied the correct methodological choices should be a key element of empirical economics. So far, such discussions remain very limited, as there are no incentives to detect potential errors in the work of others. The dominant strategy is looking generously over the shortfalls of each other's studies, with the quid pro quo that no one looks too closely at the shortfalls of one's own studies, too. No one gains anything from digging too deeply into the work of others. Open data policies alone will solve the problem surrounding the garden of forking paths only for the politically most relevant studies. For all other studies, no one has any incentives to investigate them, and we remain ignorant whether they correspond to true feedback or not.

One might object that replication is futile since the research community anyway only focuses on the very best studies, and these studies are much more likely to be true. It does therefore not matter if the majority of studies in economics constitutes false feedback, as the research community ignores them anyway. However, these very best studies are not by default more true;

they can hide large variation in feedback as well. To the contrary, we should focus on and redo these very best studies and try to estimate how much variation in feedback they produce. If we simply accept them as true without systematic assessment of how their estimates vary, we do not know how reliable they truly are.

Mere appeals to an elevated sense of morality among researchers, in the spirit of Merton's (1973) norms of science, are unlikely to yield success. Researchers respond to incentives, just like everyone else. The only realistic improvement we can pursue is aligning these incentives. Like in any other collective dilemma, the benefits of producing interesting but false studies are private, while the costs are socialized. By the same logic, if you are the only researcher who does not p-hack, you lose out against all those who do. Because the large majority of researchers (unconsciously) p-hack their results, they are able to present a series of strong and consistent results. In contrast, the studies of those researchers who refrain from p-hacking and present their results as messy as they really are will be rejected in the publication process. P-hackers thus crowd out those researchers that do not. To keep up with all others, researchers are almost forced to resort to p-hacking (see, e.g., Smaldino and McElreath 2016 about the "natural selection of bad science"). Moreover, many researchers assume that everyone else has already p-hacked their results to make them look as favorable as possible. Under this mindset, if researchers are then still not able to present a series of strong and consistent results, their studies are seen as unconvincing. We are trapped in a state of false beauty of our results.

Duvendack et al. (2015) discuss the different incentives of replicators, journal editors, and original authors with respect to replication. Much of the incentives replicators face depend on their chances to get published. They face adversity from the research community because of an alleged lack of originality, a missing own research agenda, or free-riding on the reputation of more established authors. In contrast, journal editors are concerned that replications will generate less per-page citations. They may face trouble when a fierce debate between authors of the replication and the original studies ensues. Such controversy may also alienate established authors. Most important, Duvendack et al. (2015) argue that editors may want to avoid uncovering problematic aspects of the studies published in their journal. On the other hand, publishing failed replications of popular studies may increase their journal's citation count. Journal editors may thus have an incentive to publish replication failure of popular studies published in journals competing with them. Finally, original authors will probably resist replications most fiercely. They have little upside and a large downside from replications of their work. While a replication success provides only moderate gain, a replication failure could prove fatal for the original study. The best outcome for the original authors is when everyone takes their studies at face value and does not dig too deep into the details of the study. Many authors would thus not welcome increased efforts for replication. We need to change the incentives in the research community such that the conduct of replications becomes more favorable for all of the participating agents.

To achieve this, we would need to design our institutions such that Merton's (1973) scientific norms become true by themselves. We are economists, and one of our major businesses is incentives. We are successful in designing markets, auctions, or organizations because we are well aware that suboptimal design eliciting the wrong incentives will result in collective failure. Yet in our empirical research we assume that we only have the benefit of the collective in mind. Economists take agents as self-interested. Nevertheless, under the right conditions, a beneficial outcome can still emerge. We need to view researchers as self-interested, too, and create institutions that allow for reinstating effective cooperation. The main target of such a change should be separating the execution of a study from the benefits arising from the study's outcome. However, such large-scale institutional change is an endeavor that will take decades to complete. In the short run, in contrast, there already exist some ideas how replication in economics could be fostered.

Journals could assign at least one reviewer to the task of replicating the data analysis. This reviewer's task would be to check whether the results still hold up under alternative choices of important researcher degrees of freedom. Ioannidis (2018b) even argues that "Peer review without checking data, protocols, and methods is superficial at best". The incentives of reviewers to falsify the study would not be much different from the incentives they have to criticize a study when only looking at the manuscript. Moreover, the original authors would have the possibility to defend themselves against an overly biased choice of alternative researcher degrees of freedom by the reviewers within the publication process itself.

Furthermore, fresh PhD student in empirical economics should, as their first project, pursue a replication of at least one study. Aside from learning the business of empirical research, the fresh perspective of a relative outsider and the subsequent inquiry into all relevant researcher degrees of freedom could provide a valuable contribution to the literature. Online platforms might help PhD students in discussing the adequacy of their methodological choices arising from such replications.

On a broader level, journals could start subjecting a random sample of studies published in their outlet for replication. Each randomly drawn study could be assigned to different reviewers, and if they all agree, the study would obtain a "replicated" label. If not, the ratio of "replicated versus not-replicated" could appear on the main page of the study. In any case, the replication reports would need to be attached to the study, for everyone to see them. The randomness inherent to such a policy would save costs and put everyone on equal footing. It would serve as a credible threat for researchers. If authors want to opt in for replication on their own initiative, they should be allowed so, too.

Efforts toward a "Journal of Replication Studies" (Coffman and Niederle 2015) are usually dismissed by the argument that such a journal will not enjoy the necessary status. Coffman et al. (2017) thus propose that all economic journals could have a replication section, where researcher can publish short reports. Currently, only few journals have such a section. Yet, should replication indeed become an integral part of our research culture, it will probably have its own journals dedicated to it, too.

A general problem is the incentives of the replicating researchers to falsify a study. While confirmatory evidence of an important study does not cause much repercussions, contradictory evidence catches everyone's attention. Researchers replicating studies are subject to the same biases as researchers conducting the original studies. They may use their available researcher degrees of freedom to actively search for null results. P-hacking might be replaced by null-hacking (Bryan et al. 2019). The only solution to this is that several independent researchers purse replications of the same study. If we encourage several replicators to test a given study, the truth is more likely to shine through.

Maniadis et al. (2017) investigate how biases of researchers conducting replications affect the post-study probability (PSP) that a research finding is true. They consider four scenarios: i) unbiased replication, ii) replication with a bias in line with the original results (sympathetic replications), iii) replication with a bias toward providing evidence opposing the original result (adversarial replication), and iv) a mix of these three types of replication attempts. Whereas only few adversarial replications are required to strongly increase the PSP, it requires more sympathetic replications to obtain the same increase in the PSP. Maniadis et al. (2017) therefore argue that in environments where there is an aversion to contradict the authors of initial studies, the role of replication to approach truth is diminished, and a larger number of replications is required until a result is established. In contrast, with adequate statistical power, and provided that not all of the three attempts are sympathetic replications, two successful replications out of three attempts would be sufficient to establish a high PSP.

One might argue that transparency in research could stifle scientific progress, as researchers would not be able to make extraordinary discoveries anymore, because they are afraid to commit errors. However, we achieve progress in science only when we better approach truth. Establishing false feedback as a breakthrough without thoroughly checking it helps no one except the respective authors themselves. We need to thoroughly check for potential errors in every extraordinary discovery. This is absolute key to scientific progress. We should rather address the problem that researchers face adversity when they do commit errors in their work. Committing errors should not be seen as something bad but rather as a normal consequence of risky research. Those researchers who dare to propose extraordinary discovers should actively contribute in discovering potential weakness in their arguments, such that the research community can better identify alternative ways to move forward.

Errors need to be uncovered, whatever the actual story behind them, and irrespective of whether they were made with good intentions. If replications became the norm, failed replications would become the norm, too, and those researchers, which have published nonreplicable findings, would suffer fewer damage to their reputation, as it would be seen as the normal course of science.

For instance, journals like Nature and Science have much high retraction rates than journals in economics, which almost never retract publications. It is unlikely though that economists commit less errors than natural scientists. The problem is once again that currently in economics we have great difficulties in falsifying studies. Nature and Science publish only the most extraordinary discoveries, which means that many of them incur the risk to be false. In the same manner, failed replications would be the price journals would have to pay for publishing only very unexpected studies.

Open criticism is an integral part of every science. Replication would be no different than criticism in a research seminar, with the central difference that replicators would have themselves access to the data. Otherwise, criticism continues to be based on the nicely polished surface of every publication, where all kinds of potential shortfalls remain hidden from the eyes of critics.

14.6 A culture of replication

Crucial is a change of mind in the entire profession. Replication needs to be seen as something valuable to economics, having a positive effect on the growth of scientific knowledge. If we could achieve such a change of mind, all kinds of replications would follow suit. Currently, many academic economists just bury their heads in the sand; they prefer to uphold a distorted image of economics as working perfectly, largely ignoring the existence of false feedback. However, with the transition toward open science under way, the status attributed to replications will increase. A single study will not be taken as evidence anymore, only a series of successful and sufficiently varied replications will pass this criterion.

Importantly, criticizing findings should not be taken as criticizing researchers, and failed replications should not be detrimental to the career of researchers.

In any appeal to systematic replication, the honest researchers, which have, for instance, never p-hacked, are often most offended. They have conducted solid research over many years and are now accused of something they did never even do. Yet it is the honest researchers that would profit most from systematic replication, because they could finally compete on equal grounds with those overly pragmatic researchers that always p-hack intentionally. Moreover, the absence of p-hacking is not a sufficient condition to approach true feedback. Honest researchers might have embarked on some false forking paths, too, and they could profit from replicators pointing out potential weak spots.

Concentrated initiatives toward systematic replication would have a large impact on actual scientific practice. Researchers would start thinking twice before they publish their empirical findings. If researchers operate under the knowledge that other researchers may check their chosen methodological approaches, which should be the norm in every science anyway, they will proceed much more carefully and, consequently, also more truthfully. Researchers will start publishing only those empirical findings they are convinced that they will stand up to potentially harsh replication efforts.

The systematic investigation of how variation in the garden of forking paths affects our empirical results actually has the potential to become a research field of its own. We need knowledge about when, how, and to what extent changes in researcher degrees of freedom impact results (see Young and Stewart (2020) for an example).

Importantly, what we need are high-quality replications. Otherwise, we open up the door to all kinds of ideologically motivated debunking of actually true empirical findings. This would not correspond to a step forward, but to a big step backward. It further underscores the importance of a reliable platform for high-quality replications, such as in special sections in top journals in economics.

Many researchers also fear unjustified criticism through low-quality replications. Yet just because there is a realistic danger of unfounded criticism, it does not mean that there should be no criticism at all. Thoughtless arguments will not stand a chance against reasonable arguments. We can count on a capacity for careful reasoning among the research community. Few researchers enjoy embarrassing themselves in the eyes of other researchers by producing low-quality replications.

If a study does not replicate, it is likely that neither the original authors nor the replicating authors will give in. It is notoriously difficult to change the minds of people who have stakes in a certain position. However, any debate is not intended to persuade either of the two sides, but to persuade the audience. Researchers who follow the debate and do not (yet) have stakes in either position are likely to lean toward the side with the stronger arguments. This is most important for young researchers, who will obtain relevant information about the direction they should move toward. Few young researchers aspire to walk into a field dominated by false feedback, so replication debates may at least inform young researchers transparently about potential weakness in certain popular studies.

Famous replication debates such as McCrary (2002) versus Levitt (2002), Rothstein (2007) versus Hoxby (2007), or Albouy (2012) versus Acemoglu et al. (2012) show how changes in certain researcher degrees of freedom can influence results, and how different researchers' opinions about them can be.

However, in each of these three instances, the ensuing debate made it relatively clear who has had the upper hand in the end.

If replication efforts end up in an impasse between two opposing parties, they could jointly resort to an "adversarial collaboration" (Nosek and Errington 2020b). They would need to come together and pre-commit to a specific pre-analysis plan before they even execute the study. Just like in a registered report, researchers define together the ways they intend to take through the garden of forking paths ex-ante. The broader the claims the two parties want to make about the study, the more variation they should grant the pre-analysis plan. Adversarial collaborations are a means to shift from an unproductive exchange of arguments toward a common target (Nosek and Errington 2020b).

If after repeated replication efforts a dataset turns out, in connection with a specific research design, to be laden with too much uncertainty, that is, if all of the involved researchers reach very different conclusions, this is absolutely crucial information. We need knowledge about the uncertainty inherent to our research setups. Because if these research setups do not allow us reaching any reliable conclusions, we know we have to move on to alternative datasets or research designs.

False feedback is thus also worse than no feedback, because in the latter case we are at least aware that we do not know and can prepare for this uncertainty. In case of false feedback, we only think we know, and this false certainty can lead us far astray or even move us backward.

Economics needs to distance itself from the idea that each new study constitutes a severe empirical test providing a reliable answer. What we require are repeated answers to our most important questions. There is no other way to overcome the false feedback problem than by replication, replication, and again replication. Such a paradigm change in methodology could finally spur more visible progress in economics. It would not only provide more reliable answers to our questions, but also allow detecting where we are not yet able to provide such answers, and thus identify those questions where we need to concentrate our collective research efforts on.

References

Abdi, H. (2007). Bonferroni and Šidák corrections for multiple comparisons. In N. Salkind (Ed.), Encyclopedia of Measurement and Statistics (103–107). Sage.

Abrams, E., Libgober, J., & List, J. A. (2020). Research registries: Facts, myths, and possible improvements. National Bureau of Economic Research, No. 27250.

Acemoglu, D., Johnson, S., & Robinson, J. A. (2012). The colonial origins of comparative development: An empirical investigation: Reply. American Economic Review, 102(6), 3077–3110.

Akerlof, G. (1970). The market for "lemons": Quality uncertainty and the market mechanism. The Quarterly Journal of Economics, 84(3): 488–500.

Akerlof, G. A., & Michaillat, P. (2018). Persistence of false paradigms in low-power sciences. Proceedings of the National Academy of Sciences, 115(52), 13228–13233.

Albouy, D. Y. (2012). The colonial origins of comparative development: An empirical investigation: Comment. American Economic Review, 102(6), 3059–3076.

Andrews, I., & Kasy, M. (2019). Identification of and correction for publication bias. American Economic Review, 109(8), 2766–2794.

Angrist, J. D., & Pischke, J. S. (2010). The credibility revolution in empirical economics: How better research design is taking the con out of econometrics. Journal of Economic Perspectives, 24(2), 3–30.

Angrist, J. D., & Pischke, J. S. (2008). Mostly harmless econometrics: An empiricist's companion. Princeton University Press.

Baker, M. (2016). Reproducibility crisis? Nature, 533(26), 353–366.

Bargh, J. A., Chen, M., & Burrows, L. (1996). Automaticity of social behavior: Direct effects of trait construct and stereotype activation on action. Journal of Personality and Social Psychology, 71(2), 230–244.

Bédécarrats, F., Guérin, I., Morvant-Roux, S., & Roubaud, F. (2019). Estimating microcredit impact with low take-up, contamination and inconsistent data. A replication study of Crépon, Devoto, Duflo, and Parienté (American Economic Journal: Applied Economics, 2015). International Journal for Re-Views in Empirical Economics (IREE), 3(2019–3), 1–22.

Bem, D. J. (2011). Feeling the future: experimental evidence for anomalous retroactive influences on cognition and affect. Journal of Personality and Social Psychology, 100(3), 407–425.

Benjamin, D. J., Berger, J. O., Johannesson, M., Nosek, B. A., Wagenmakers, E. J., Berk, R., ... & Cesarini, D. (2018). Redefine statistical significance. Nature Human Behaviour, 2(1), 6–10.

Benjamini, Y., & Hochberg, Y. (1995). Controlling the false discovery rate: A practical and powerful approach to multiple testing. Journal of the Royal Statistical Society: Series B (Methodological), 57(1), 289–300.

Benjamini, Y., & Yekutieli, D. (2001). The control of the false discovery rate in multiple testing under dependency. Annals of Statistics, 29(4), 1165–1188.

Bettis, R. A. (2012). The search for asterisks: Compromised statistical tests and flawed theories. Strategic Management Journal, 33(1), 108–113.

Biddle, J. E., & Hamermesh, D. S. (2017). Theory and measurement: Emergence, consolidation, and erosion of a consensus. History of Political Economy, 49(Supplement), 34–57.

Black, B. S., Desai, H., Litvak, K., Yoo, W., & Yu, J. J. (2020). Specification choice in randomized and natural experiments: Lessons from the regulation SHO experiment. Northwestern Law & Econ Research Paper Forthcoming.

Borges, J. L. (1941). The garden of forking paths. Fictions.

Brodeur, A., Cook, N., & Heyes, A. (2020). Methods matter: P-hacking and publication bias in causal analysis in economics. American Economic Review, 110(11), 3634–3660.

Brodeur, A., Lé, M., Sangnier, M., & Zylberberg, Y. (2016). Star wars: The empirics strike back. American Economic Journal: Applied Economics, 8(1), 1–32.

Bryan, C. J., Yeager, D. S., & O'Brien, J. M. (2019). Replicator degrees of freedom allow publication of misleading failures to replicate. Proceedings of the National Academy of Sciences, 116(51), 25535–25545.

Camerer, C. F., Dreber, A., Forsell, E., Ho, T. H., Huber, J., Johannesson, M., ... & Heikensten, E. (2016). Evaluating replicability of laboratory experiments in economics. Science, 351(6280), 1433–1436.

Camerer, C. F., Dreber, A., Holzmeister, F., Ho, T. H., Huber, J., Johannesson, M., ... & Altmejd, A. (2018). Evaluating the replicability of social science experiments in Nature and Science between 2010 and 2015. Nature Human Behaviour, 2(9), 637.

Chakravartty, A. (2017). Scientific realism. In E. Zalta (Ed.), The Stanford encyclopedia of philosophy. https://plato.stanford.edu/archives/sum2017/entries/scientific-realism.

Chalmers, A. F. (2013). What is this thing called science? (4th ed.). Hackett Publishing.

Chambers, C. (2019). What's next for registered reports? Nature, 573(7773), 187–189.

Chang, A. C., & Li, P. (2017). A preanalysis plan to replicate sixty economics research papers that worked half of the time. American Economic Review, 107(5), 60–64.

Card, D., DellaVigna, S., & Malmendier, U. (2011). The role of theory in field experiments. Journal of Economic Perspectives, 25(3), 39–62.

Card, D., & Krueger, A. B. (1995). Time-series minimum-wage studies: A meta-analysis. The American Economic Review, 85(2), 238–243.

Clemens, M. A. (2017). The meaning of failed replications: A review and proposal. Journal of Economic Surveys, 31(1), 326–342.

Christensen, G., Freese, J., & Miguel, E. (2019). Transparent and reproducible social science research: How to do open science. University of California Press.

Christensen, G., & Miguel, E. (2018). Transparency, reproducibility, and the credibility of economics research. Journal of Economic Literature, 56(3), 920–980.

Christensen, G., Wang, Z., Levy Paluck, E., Swanson, N., Birke, D., Miguel, E., & Littman, R. (2020). Open science practices are on the rise: The state of social science (3S) survey. CEGA Working Paper Series.

Coffman, L. C., & Niederle, M. (2015). Pre-analysis plans have limited upside, especially where replications are feasible. Journal of Economic Perspectives, 29(3), 81–98.

Coffman, L. C., Niederle, M., & Wilson, A. J. (2017). A proposal to organize and promote replications. American Economic Review, 107(5), 41–45.

Colquhoun, D. (2014). An investigation of the false discovery rate and the misinterpretation of p-values. Royal Society Open Science, 1(3), 140216.

Colquhoun, D. (2017). The reproducibility of research and the misinterpretation of p-values. Royal Society Open Science, 4(12), 171085.

Crépon, B., Devoto, F., Duflo, E., & Parienté, W. (2015). Estimating the impact of microcredit on those who take it up: Evidence from a randomized experiment in Morocco. American Economic Journal: Applied Economics, 7(1), 123–150.

David, M. (2016). The correspondence theory of truth. In E. Zalta (Ed.), The Stanford encyclopedia of philosophy. https://plato.stanford.edu/archives/fall2016/entries/truth-correspondence.

De Long, J. B., & Lang, K. (1992). Are all economic hypotheses false? Journal of Political Economy, 100(6), 1257–1272.

Denton, F. T. (1985). Data mining as an industry. The Review of Economics and Statistics, 67(1), 124–127.

Doucouliagos, C., & Stanley, T. D. (2013). Are all economic facts greatly exaggerated? Theory competition and selectivity. Journal of Economic Surveys, 27(2), 316–339.

Doyle, A. C. (1914). The valley of fear. Project Gutenberg.

Duhem, P. (1906/1976). Physical theory and experiment. In S. Harding (Ed.), Can theories be refuted?: Essays on the Duhem-Quine thesis. (pp. 1–40). Springer.

Duvendack, M., Palmer-Jones, R. W., & Reed, W. R. (2015). Replications in economics: A progress report. Econ Journal Watch, 12(2), 164–191.

Fafchamps, M., & Labonne, J. (2017). Using split samples to improve inference on causal effects. Political Analysis, 25(4), 465–482.

Franco, A., Malhotra, N., & Simonovits, G. (2014). Publication bias in the social sciences: Unlocking the file drawer. Science, 345(6203), 1502–1505.

Frey, B. S., & Iselin, D. (Eds.). (2017). Economic ideas you should forget. Springer.

Gelman, A. (2020). Econ grad student asks, "why is the government paying us money, instead of just firing us all?" https://statmodeling.stat.columbia.edu.

Gelman, A. (2018). The failure of null hypothesis significance testing when studying incremental changes, and what to do about it. Personality and Social Psychology Bulletin, 44(1), 16–23.

Gelman, A. (2017). The piranha problem in social psychology/behavioral economics: The "take a pill" model of science eats itself. https://statmodeling.stat.columbia.edu.

Gelman, A. (2013). Does it matter that a sample is unrepresentative? It depends on the size of the treatment interactions. https://statmodeling.stat.columbia.edu.

Gelman, A., & Carlin, J. (2014). Beyond power calculations: Assessing type S (sign) and type M (magnitude) errors. Perspectives on Psychological Science, 9(6), 641–651.

Gelman, A., & Loken, E. (2013). The garden of forking paths: Why multiple comparisons can be a problem, even when there is no "fishing expedition" or "p-hacking" and the research hypothesis was posited ahead of time. Department of Statistics, Columbia University, 348.

Gelman, A., & Vehtari, A. (2020). What are the most important statistical ideas of the past 50 years? arXiv preprint: 2012.00174.

Gertler, P., Galiani, S., & Romero, M. (2018). How to make replication the norm. Nature 554(7693), 417–419.

Gilles, G. (2014). Picketty findings undercut by errors. Financial Times.

Grimes, D. R., Bauch, C. T., & Ioannidis, J. P. (2018). Modelling science trustworthiness under publish or perish pressure. Royal Society Open Science, 5(1), 171511.

Hardwicke, T. E., & Ioannidis, J. P. (2018). Mapping the universe of registered reports. Nature Human Behaviour, 2(11), 793–796.

Hardwicke, T. E., Serghiou, S., Janiaud, P., Danchev, V., Crüwell, S., Goodman, S. N., & Ioannidis, J. P. (2019). Calibrating the scientific ecosystem through meta-research. Annual Review of Statistics and its Application, 7(1), 11–37.

Harvey, C. R., Liu, Y., & Zhu, H. (2016). … and the cross-section of expected returns. The Review of Financial Studies, 29(1), 5–68.

Hayek, F. A. (1973). Law, legislation and liberty. Vol. 1: Rules and order. Routledge.

Hayek, F. V. (1943). Scientism and the study of society. Part II. Economica, 10(37), 34–63.

Hendry, D. F., & Krolzig, H. M. (2004). We ran one regression. Oxford Bulletin of Economics and Statistics, 66(5), 799–810.

Herndon, T., Ash, M., & Pollin, R. (2014). Does high public debt consistently stifle economic growth? A critique of Reinhart and Rogoff. Cambridge Journal of Economics, 38(2), 257–279.

Hoover, K. D., & Perez, S. J. (2004). Truth and robustness in cross-country growth regressions. Oxford Bulletin of Economics and Statistics, 66(5), 765–798.

Hoxby, C. M. (2007). Does competition among public schools benefit students and taxpayers?: Reply. American Economic Review, 97(5), 2038–2055.

Hubbard, R. (2015). Corrupt research: The case for reconceptualizing empirical management and social science. Sage.

Hubbard, R., & Lindsay, R. M. (2013a). From significant difference to significant sameness: Proposing a paradigm shift in business research. Journal of Business Research, 66(9), 1377–1388.

Hubbard, R., & Lindsay, R. M. (2013b). The significant difference paradigm promotes bad science. Journal of Business Research, 66(9), 1393–1397.

Ioannidis, J. P. (2019). The importance of predefined rules and prespecified statistical analyses: Do not abandon significance. JAMA, 321(21), 2067–2068.

Ioannidis, J. P. (2018a). The proposal to lower P value thresholds to .005. JAMA, 319(14), 1429–1430.

Ioannidis, J. P. (2018b). Why replication has more scientific value than original discovery. Behavioral and Brain Sciences, 41, 27.

Ioannidis, J. P. (2012). Why science is not necessarily self-correcting. Perspectives on Psychological Science, 7(6), 645–654.

Ioannidis, J. P. (2005). Why most published research findings are false. PLOS Medicine, 2(8), e124.

Ioannidis, J. P., Stanley, T. D., & Doucouliagos, H. (2017). The power of bias in economics research. Economic Journal, 127(605), 236–265.

John, L. K., Loewenstein, G., & Prelec, D. (2012). Measuring the prevalence of questionable research practices with incentives for truth telling. Psychological Science, 23(5), 524–532.

Kahneman, D. (2011). Thinking, fast and slow. Macmillan.

Kerr, N. L. (1998). HARKing: Hypothesizing after the results are known. Personality and Social Psychology Review, 2(3), 196–217.

Keynes, J. M. (1940). On a method of statistical business-cycle research: A comment. The Economic Journal, 50(197), 154–156.

Klein, R. A., Ratliff, K. A., Vianello, M., Adams Jr, R. B., Bahník, Š., Bernstein, M. J., ... & Cemalcilar, Z. (2014). Investigating variation in replicability. Social Psychology, 45(3), 142–152.

Klein, R. A., Vianello, M., Hasselman, F., Adams, B. G., Adams Jr, R. B., Alper, S., ... & Batra, R. (2018). Many Labs 2: Investigating variation in replicability across samples and settings. Advances in Methods and Practices in Psychological Science, 1(4), 443–490.

Kuhn, T. S. (1962). The structure of scientific revolutions. University of Chicago Press.

LaCour, M. J., & Green, D. P. (2014). When contact changes minds: An experiment on transmission of support for gay equality. Science, 346(6215), 1366–1369.

Lakatos, I. (1970). Falsification and the methodology of scientific research programmes. In I. Lakatos, A. Musgrave (Eds.), Criticism and the growth of knowledge (pp. 170–196). Cambridge University Press.

Leamer, E. E. (1985). Sensitivity analyses would help. The American Economic Review, 75(3), 308–313.

Leamer, E. E. (1983). Let's take the con out of econometrics. The American Economic Review, 73(1), 31–43.

Leamer, E. E. (1978). Specification searches: Ad hoc inference with nonexperimental data (Vol. 53). John Wiley & Sons Incorporated.

Levitt, S. D. (2002). Using electoral cycles in police hiring to estimate the effects of police on crime: Reply. American Economic Review, 92(4), 1244–1250.

Levitt, S. D., & Dubner, S. J. (2005). Freakonomics: A rogue economist explores the hidden side of everything. Harper Collins.

List, J. A., Shaikh, A. M., & Xu, Y. (2019). Multiple hypothesis testing in experimental economics. Experimental Economics, 22(4), 773–793.

Lovell, M. (1983). Data mining. The Review of Economics and Statistics, 65(1), 1–12.

Lowenstein, R. (2001). When genius failed – The rise and fall of long-term capital management. Harper Collins.

Maniadis, Z., Tufano, F., & List, J. A. (2017). To replicate or not to replicate? Exploring reproducibility in economics through the lens of a model and a pilot study. The Economic Journal, 127(605): 209–235.

Mayo, D. G. (1996a). Ducks, rabbits, and normal science: Recasting the Kuhn's-eye view of Popper's demarcation of science. The British Journal for the Philosophy of Science, 47(2), 271–290.

Mayo, D. G. (1996b). Error and the growth of experimental knowledge. University of Chicago Press.

McCloskey, D. N., Ziliak, S. T. (2004). Size matters: The standard error of regressions in the American Economic Review. The Journal of Socio-Economics, 33(5), 527–546.

McCloskey, D. N., & Ziliak, S. T. (1996). The standard error of regressions. Journal of Economic Literature, 34(1), 97–114.

McCrary, J. (2002). Using electoral cycles in police hiring to estimate the effect of police on crime: Comment. American Economic Review, 92(4), 1236–1243.

McShane, B. B., Gal, D., Gelman, A., Robert, C., & Tackett, J. L. (2019a). Abandon statistical significance. The American Statistician, 73(sup1), 235–245.

McShane, B. B., Tackett, J. L., Böckenholt, U., & Gelman, A. (2019b). Large-scale replication projects in contemporary psychological research. The American Statistician, 73(sup1), 99–105.

Meehl, P. E. (1978). Theoretical risks and tabular asterisks: Sir Karl, Sir Ronald, and the slow progress of soft psychology. Journal of Consulting and Clinical Psychology, 46(4), 806.

Merton, R. K. (1973). The sociology of science: Theoretical and empirical investigations. University of Chicago press.

Miguel, E., Camerer, C., Casey, K., Cohen, J., Esterling, K. M., Gerber, A., ... & Laitin, D. (2014). Promoting transparency in social science research. Science, 343(6166), 30–31.

Mueller-Langer, F., Fecher, B., Harhoff, D., & Wagner, G. G. (2019). Replication studies in economics – How many and which papers are chosen for replication, and why? Research Policy, 48(1), 62–83.

Necker, S. (2014). Scientific misbehavior in economics. Research Policy, 43(10), 1747–1759.

Nelder, J. (1986). Statistics, science and technology (with discussion). Journal of the Royal Statistical Society: Series A (General), 149(2), 109–121.

Nelson, R. R. (2008). Bounded rationality, cognitive maps, and trial and error learning. Journal of Economic Behavior and Organization, 67(1), 78–89.

Nelson, R. R. (2003). On the uneven evolution of human know-how. Research Policy, 32(6), 909–922.

Neumark, D. (2001). The employment effects of minimum wages: Evidence from a prespecified research design the employment effects of minimum wages. Industrial Relations: A Journal of Economy and Society, 40(1), 121–144.

Nickerson, R. S. (1998). Confirmation bias: A ubiquitous phenomenon in many guises. Review of General Psychology, 2(2), 175–220.

Nissen, S. B., Magidson, T., Gross, K., & Bergstrom, C. T. (2016). Publication bias and the canonization of false facts. Elife, 5, e21451.

Nosek, B. A., & Errington, T. M. (2020a). What is replication? PLOS Biology, 18(3), e3000691.

Nosek, B. A., Ebersole, C. R., DeHaven, A. C., & Mellor, D. T. (2018). The preregistration revolution. Proceedings of the National Academy of Sciences, 115(11), 2600–2606.

Nosek, B. A., & Errington, T. M. (2020b). The best time to argue about what a replication means? Before you do it. Nature, 583(7817), 518–520.

Nosek, B. A., Spies, J. R., & Motyl, M. (2012). Scientific utopia: II. Restructuring incentives and practices to promote truth over publishability. Perspectives on Psychological Science, 7(6), 615–631.

Open Science Collaboration. (2015). Estimating the reproducibility of psychological science. Science, 349(6251), aac4716.

Plato (1892). Meno. (B. Jowett, Trans.). Random House.

Plato (1888). The republic of Plato. (B. Jowett, Trans.). Macmillan.

Platt, J. R. (1964). Strong inference. Science, 146(3642), 347–353.

Popper, K. R. (1945). The open society and its enemies. Routledge Classics.

Popper, K. R. (1957). The poverty of historicism. Routledge Classics.

Popper, K. R. (1959). The logic of scientific discovery. Routledge Classics.

Popper, K. R. (1963). Conjectures and refutations: The growth of scientific knowledge. Routledge Classics.

Popper, K. R. (1972). Objective knowledge: An evolutionary approach. Oxford University Press.

Popper, K. R. (1976). Background knowledge and scientific growth. In S. Harding (Ed.), Can theories be refuted? Essays on the Duhem-Quine thesis. (pp. 113–115). Springer.

Popper, K. R. (1985). Evolutionary epistemology. In Open questions in quantum physics (pp. 395–413). Springer.

Popper, K. R. (1994). All life is problem solving. Routledge.

Quine, W. V. (1951). Main trends in recent philosophy: Two dogmas of empiricism. The Philosophical Review, 60(1), 20–43.

Reinhart, C. M., & Rogoff, K. S. (2010). Growth in a time of debt. American Economic Review, 100(2), 573–578.

Reiss, J. (2008). Error in economics: Towards a more evidence–based methodology. Routledge.

Retraction Watch (2020). Tracking retractions as a window into the scientific process. wwww.retrationwatch.com.

Rosenthal, R. (1979). The file drawer problem and tolerance for null results. Psychological Bulletin, 86(3), 638.

Rothstein, J. (2007). Does competition among public schools benefit students and taxpayers?: Comment. American Economic Review, 97(5), 2026–2037.

Russell, B. (1956). Logic and knowledge: Essays 1901–1950. Routledge.

Russell, B. (1923). Vagueness. The Australasian Journal of Psychology and Philosophy, 1(2), 84–92.

Sala-i-Martin, X. (1997). I just ran two million regressions. American Economic Review, 87(2), 178–183.

Schimmack, U., Heene, M., & Kesavan, K. (2017). Reconstruction of a train wreck: How priming research went off the rails. https://replicationindex.com/2017/02/02/reconstruction-of-a-train-wreck-how-priming-research-went-of-the-rails/.

Schimmack, U. (2012). The ironic effect of significant results on the credibility of multiple-study articles. Psychological Methods, 17(4), 551.

Sextus Empiricus (1990). Outline of Pyrrhonism. (R.G. Bury, Trans.). Prometheus Books.

Silberzahn, R., & Uhlmann, E. L. (2015). Crowdsourced research: Many hands make tight work. Nature News, 526(7572), 189.

Silberzahn, R., Uhlmann, E. L., Martin, D. P., Anselmi, P., Aust, F., Awtrey, E., ... & Carlsson, R. (2018). Many analysts, one data set: Making transparent how variations in analytic choices affect results. Advances in Methods and Practices in Psychological Science, 1(3), 337–356.

Simmons, J. P., Nelson, L. D., & Simonsohn, U. (2011). False-positive psychology: Undisclosed flexibility in data collection and analysis allows presenting anything as significant. Psychological Science, 22(11), 1359–1366.

Simonsohn (2020). P-hacking fast and slow: Evaluating a forthcoming AER paper deeming some econ literatures less trustworthy. http://datacolada.org/91.

Simonsohn (2016). P-hacked hypotheses are deceivingly robust. http://datacolada.org/48.

Simonsohn, U., Nelson, L. D., & Simmons, J. P. (2019). P-curve won't do your laundry, but it will distinguish replicable from non-replicable findings in observational research: Comment on Bruns & Ioannidis (2016). PLOS One, 14(3), e0213454.

Simonsohn, U., Nelson, L. D., & Simmons, J. P. (2014). P-curve: A key to the file-drawer. Journal of Experimental Psychology: General, 143(2), 534.

Simonsohn, U., Simmons, J. P., & Nelson, L. D. (2020). Specification curve analysis. Nature Human Behaviour, 4(11), 1208–1214.

Smaldino, P. E., & McElreath, R. (2016). The natural selection of bad science. Royal Society Open Science, 3(9), 160384.

Stanley, T. D., & Doucouliagos, H. (2014). Meta-regression approximations to reduce publication selection bias. Research Synthesis Methods, 5(1), 60–78.

Steegen, S., Tuerlinckx, F., Gelman, A., & Vanpaemel, W. (2016). Increasing transparency through a multiverse analysis. Perspectives on Psychological Science, 11(5), 702–712.

Sterling, T. D. (1959). Publication decisions and their possible effects on inferences drawn from tests of significance – Or vice versa. Journal of the American statistical association, 54(285), 30–34.

Sukhtankar, S. (2017). Replications in development economics. American Economic Review, 107(5), 32–36.

Taleb, N. N. (2018). Skin in the game: Hidden asymmetries in daily life. Random House.

Taleb, N. N. (2016). A short note on P-value hacking. arXiv preprint: 1603.07532.

Taleb, N. N. (2012). Antifragile: Things that gain from disorder. Random House.

Taleb, N. N. (2007). The black swan: The impact of the highly improbable. Random House.

Taleb, N. N. (2001). Fooled by randomness: The hidden role of chance in life and in the markets. Random House.

Tversky, A., & Kahneman, D. (1971). Belief in the law of small numbers. Psychological Bulletin, 76(2), 105.

Vilhuber, L. (2019, May). Report by the AEA Data Editor. AEA Papers and Proceedings, 109, 718–729.

Wagenmakers, E. J., Wetzels, R., Borsboom, D., van der Maas, H. L., & Kievit, R. A. (2012). An agenda for purely confirmatory research. Perspectives on Psychological Science, 7(6), 632–638.

Wasserstein, R. L., & Lazar, N. A. (2016). The ASA's statement on p-values: Context, process, and purpose. The American Statistician, 70(2), 129–133.

Wasserstein, R. L., Schirm, A. L., & Lazar, N. A. (2019). Moving to a world beyond "p< 0.05". The American Statistician, 73(sup1), 1–19.

Wells, G. L., & Windschitl, P. D. (1999). Stimulus sampling and social psychological experimentation. Personality and Social Psychology Bulletin, 25(9), 1115–1125.

Westling, T. (2011). Male organ and economic growth: Does size matter? HECER Discussion Paper No. 335.

White, H. (2000). A reality check for data snooping. Econometrica, 68(5), 1097–1126.

Wicherts, J. M., Veldkamp, C. L., Augusteijn, H. E., Bakker, M., Van Aert, R., & Van Assen, M. A. (2016). Degrees of freedom in planning, running, analyzing, and reporting psychological studies: A checklist to avoid p-hacking. Frontiers in Psychology, 7, 1832.

Wuchty, S., Jones, B. F., & Uzzi, B. (2007). The increasing dominance of teams in production of knowledge. Science, 316(5827), 1036–1039.

Yarkoni, Tal. (2019). The generalizability crisis. PsyArXiv preprint.

Young, A. (2019). Consistency without inference: Instrumental variables in practical application. London School of Economics.

Young, C., & Stewart, S. A. (2020). Multiverse analysis: Advancements for functional form robustness. Working Paper.

Zwaan, R. A., Etz, A., Lucas, R. E., & Donnellan, M. B. (2018). Making replication mainstream. Behavioral and Brain Sciences, 41, 1–50.

Index

Printed in the United States
by Baker & Taylor Publisher Services